- - - - - - - - - - *Main Street of the Northwest*

NORTHERN PACIFIC
Color Pictorial
Volume 1

by Joseph W. Shine

- Acknowledgements -

I would like to extend my sincere thanks to all of those who have helped with the preparation of this book. First of all a thank you to Ed Kanak, who contributed much of the early preparatory work. Once again I would like to thank Ernie Towler for his original art work decorating our title page. Gary Wildung who helped gain valuable rosters and data sheets from the Minnesota Historical Society. Gary Tarbox and Pat Egan who helped get the word out to the Northern Pacific Railway Historical Association. I especially would like to thank each photographer for contributing the art of their camera work. Each photographer, when known, is credited along with their respective photo. I would also like to thank those who made their collections available for all to share. They are also listed along with the particular photograph. Notice the names following each photograph - those are the people we would all like to thank.

- Dedication -

I would like to dedicate this volume to a man who was an official brakeman and conductor for the Northern Pacific Ry. He was also an unofficial public relations man for the railway. (The NP, not the BN.) He and his wife remain the unofficial promoters for the great City of Livingston, Montana.
My New Friends,

Bernice and Warren McGee

- Credits -

Front Cover Photo: NP FTs 5408A+B together with a pair of F7s form a classic A-B-B-A locomotive combination on the point of a 125-car freight near Garrison, under a beautiful Montana sky on August 15, 1957. *John Harrigan*

Title Page: The original art piece drawn by Ernie Towler, based on a photograph by Warren McGee, depicts crew members inspecting a pair of brand new Alco RS-3s road-switchers assigned to helper service on Bozeman Pass. Meanwhile a steam powered freight is being serviced at Bozeman during the last days of steam in April 1955.

Rear Cover Photo: On February 19, 1956, one of Northern Pacific's giant 4-6-6-4 locomotives, #5126, gets an eastbound with 113-cars/6,000 tons underway from Livingston bound for Laurel, Montana - nearly 100 miles away. It's a calm day at Livingston, the temperature hovers at 20-degrees above, and the big Challenger-type locomotive needs only to accelerate to 55 MPH, while the drifting throttle will keep the train rolling down the Yellowstone River Valley's grades of .3 to .59%. *Warren McGee*

⇨ ⇨

- Typesetting and Layout by Four Ways West Publications -
- Printing and Color Separations by Orange County Color Graphics, Anaheim, CA -

Four Ways West

P U B L I C A T I O N S

P.O. Box 1734 - B
La Mirada, CA 90637-1734

ISBN 0-9616874-9-5

NORTHERN PACIFIC

Color Pictorial - Volume 1

- TABLE OF CONTENTS -

Acknowledgements 2

Northern Pacific's Monad 4

The Story of the Monad 5

Foreword 6

- 1955 DIVISION LOCOMOTIVE ASSIGNMENTS -

Lake Superior Division 8

Saint Paul Division 22

Fargo Division 46

Yellowstone Division 52

Rocky Mountain Division 78

Idaho Division 94

Tacoma Division 106

- 1955 LOCOMOTIVE ROSTERS -

Passenger - EMD F-3, F-5, F-7, FP-7, F-9 36

Freight - EMD F-3, F-5, F-7 66

Freight - EMD FT, F-3, F-5, F-7, F-9 (Pictorial Roster) 76

Road Switcher - EMD GP7 102

Freight - EMD FT 116

Northern Pacific - Steam Locomotive 128

Why does the Korean flag look so familiar?

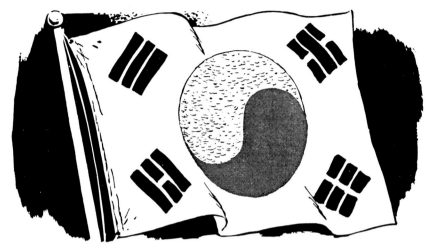

MAYBE YOU'VE NEVER seen it before. Even so, the flag of the Korean Republic —waving over Korean battlefields beside the United Nations banner—may seem strangely familiar. Northern Pacific can tell you why. Long before the Korean war, NP "borrowed" the central design, or "Monad", of this very flag for the railroad trademark. We saw it at the 1893 World's Fair in Chicago . . . adapted it . . . and adopted it for NP use. Since then, the Monad—known in the Far East as a good-luck charm—has become known in America as a sign of good transportation.

TODAY, RUSHING WAR GOODS and soldiers to danger spots is a tall transportation order for U.S. railroads—including NP. So is the big job of helping to develop America's military muscle at home. But thanks to its own 10-year "mobilization"— a giant $150-million rebuilding program just completed—Northern Pacific is better equipped than ever to serve the nation's needs. Actually, we want to do *more* than handle our war duty well. We want to keep doing a bang-up transportation job for industry, agriculture and all the folks along the "Main Street of the Northwest."

During the late 1940's and 1950's, most of the free world became acquainted with the design on the flag of the Korean Republic - the Monad. This design had been familiar with Americans and Canadians for years as the herald adopted by the Northern Pacific Ry. This advertisement appeared in magazines in late 1949 and 1950.

ROUTE OF THE *Streamlined* **NORTH COAST LIMITED**

NORTHERN PACIFIC RAILWAY

Main Street of the Northwest

At the Chicago World's Fair of 1893, E. H. McHenry, then Chief Engineer of the Northern Pacific, chanced to visit the Korean exhibit. Seeing the Korean flag, he was impressed by the simple but striking design it carried. At that time NP was searching for a suitable trademark, and Mr. McHenry realized almost immediately that this symbol could be adapted quite readily for that purpose. When he returned to St. Paul, he submitted his idea to Charles Fee, then General Passenger Agent, and together they worked out the emblem which became familiar to millions of Americans and Canadians.

Curious about the origin of this symbol, Mr. McHenry began an investigation of its history. The information he sought was difficult to find, but from a number of sources - missionaries to China, students of the Oriental philosophy - a reasonably accurate history of the Monad was finally pieced together.

What the Monad means

Although it is displayed on the Korean Flag, the Monad symbol originated in China. Variations of it have been found in several other countries including North America, where the design has appeared in Pueblo Indian pottery and in bead work of American Plains Indians. The more modern form of the Monad was introduced in the 11th century by a Chinese philosopher, Chow Lien Ki. It was used by him to illustrate a 4000-year-old philosophy which he followed.

According to this philosophy, the primary force in the universe is a sort of impersonal "nature" rather than a personified deity or "god". These teachings hold that the Illimitable (probably "nature") produced the Great Extreme (the "creative" principle). From the Great Extreme came the Two Principles, or Dual Powers, and from the Two Principles the rest of the world is descended.

For the present explanation, which is of course greatly oversimplified, it is enough to say that these Two Principles are called the Yang and the Yin. Their primitive meanings were: Yang-Light; Yin-Darkness. Philosophically, they stood for the positive and the negative. Further and later interpretations, and there are many, assigned them the meanings of force and matter, motion and rest Heaven and Earth, male and female. At present this symbol is most commonly understood in the latter sense.

Following this line of reasoning, the Chinese in their language have assigned a masculine or feminine gender to every object in nature and to numbers as well. Fire, for example, is masculine.

So are the sun, the day and odd numbers. Water, the moon, the night and even numbers are feminine.

In China, the Monad's two comma-shaped halves represent the Two Principles, the Yang and the Yin. Colors are apparently of minor importance, as the device can be found in red and black, white and black, red and green and other combinations. The original Chinese version includes a small dark dot in the light portion and a light dot in the darker half.

From Korea to America

In Korea, the Monad is quite similar to the original Chinese version and has much of the same philosophical meaning. Its colors, however, are red and blue, and it is called the "Tah-Gook". A free translation of the Oriental name of this country, Chosen, is "land of the morning calm". To Koreans, red is the royal color and blue is the color of the East or morning. Thus the "Tah-Gook" - on the flag of the Korean republic which is recognized by the United Nations - means also "kingdom of the morning".

The four additional symbols carried in the corners of this flag are called the Four Figures. Derived from the same Chinese philosophy which uses the Monad, they have many meanings.

From the arrangements of the bars, a number of moral lessons may be drawn. The weaker (short bars) should be protected by the stronger (long bars); but the more precious (long bars) should be protected by the less valuable (short bars). Like should associate with like, as shown by the three long bars in one group and the six short bars in another, but tolerance should permit the mixture of the unlike, as in the two other groups.

The Monad symbol, with the variations of the Four figures surrounding it, is quite frequently used by the Chinese as a charm to ward off evil influences and it is an important accessory to fortune-tellers and mystics. Smaller Monads may be carried about and larger ones are often hung over doorways of homes or places of business.

The Japanese version of this symbol, the "futatsu tomoe", is composed of three comma-shaped pieces inside the circle. The device is also used in that country as a good-luck token. It is most frequently made about the size of a half-dollar and quite often is carried in the sleeve of a robe.

So it is, then, that in the Orient this ancient design has become the symbol of good luck. And in America - on Northern Pacific diesels, passenger cars, freight cars, stationary and traffic office windows - it became the sign of good rail transportation.   From NP's "The Story of the Monad"

- Foreword -

Northern Pacific Color Pictorial - Volume 1, continues Four Ways West Publication's extensive coverage of the predecessor railroads which were combined to create the Burlington Northern in March 1970.

The Northern Pacific Railway Co. was the first to lay its rails from St. Paul in the northern Midwest to the shores of Puget Sound - "The Northern Route". A Bill rendering Land Grants to aid in the construction of a railroad and telegraph line was granted by the United States Congress in 1864. This Bill was similar to the one which created the First Transcontinental Railroad, the Union Pacific and Central Pacific, which was completed in May 1869. Thus, the "Northern Route" became the second Transcontinental Railroad, though not nearly as celebrated. It was opened to through traffic in 1883.

The motive power of the early Northern Pacific was the same as on any other railroad of the day, small 0-4-0s and 4-4-0s. These wheel arrangements led to larger 0-6-0s for switching and 4-6-0s for passenger and freight service. During the early part of the 20th century the road pioneered in developing the 4-6-2 and Mallet 2-6-6-2 locomotives. The NP was also the first Class I railroad to develop and purchase the popular 2-8-2 wheel arrangement. The 2-8-2 became the backbone of the NP as they were used in local service on branch lines and in heavy freight service on the main lines. They were used in helper service as well as passenger locomotives on heavy troop trains. They remained in service until the very last days of steam. There are many photos in this book of these 2-8-2's in their last years of operation.

The Northern Pacific Ry. was a pioneering company engaged in rebuilding and modernizing existing steam locomotives. The railroad was also an innovator. During the years after World War I, most railroads, including the NP, wanted to operate fewer trains, but with more tonnage. Of course, this demanded larger, more powerful locomotives. In its quest for this power, the Northern Pacific developed the first 4-8-4 locomotive, a type which became synonymous with fast passenger service. It was no coincidence that the 4-8-4 wheel arrangement became known as the "Northern" type. These locomotives became NP's A-Class and in time replaced the "standard" passenger 4-6-2 Q-Class engines. Also during the late 1920's, the NP purchased the world's largest articulated steam locomotives, the Z-5 Class 2-8-8-4's. Their reign as the world's largest stood for many years. The NP originally put these big steamers to work on the Yellowstone Division on the undulating trackage between Mandan and Glendive, through the Bad Lands, thus the 2-8-8-4 wheel arrangement became known as the Yellowstone type.

Through the decade of the 1930s and into the early 1940s, the Northern Pacific perfected their 4-8-4 type and purchased forty-seven modern articulated 4-6-6-4's, nearly identical with Union Pacific's famous Challenger types.

For their size, the NP had a much more modern steam locomotive fleet during the late 1930's and 1940's, than most larger roads.

In-as-much as production of the FT began in November 1939, many contended that the Northern Pacific was a late advocate of the diesel road locomotive, opting to purchase their first EMD FT diesels during 1944 and early 1945. Consider that two other large Western roads, Union Pacific and Southern Pacific, did not even purchase diesel road locomotives until the advent of the F3 in mid-1945. However, the NP was an early customer of EMD's F3, purchasing both passenger and freight versions. The railroad also purchased late model F3 locomotives. These machines were much more sophisticated than their early F3s, and the NP unofficially designated them as model F5.

During dieseldom's first generation, Northern Pacific, unlike many of their neighbors and competitors, purchased only Electro-Motive Division diesel road passenger and freight locomotives, rejecting models of Alco, Baldwin and Fairbanks-Morse. The NP also opted for four-axle passenger locomotives, learning from the lessons and grief gained by the Great Northern and Southern Pacific by operating EMD E-7s in mountainous territory. The GN eventually opted for passenger F3s and F7s, while the SP put Alco's six-axle PAs to work in the Cascades.

It was a different story concerning diesel switchers, however, as models were tested and purchased from several manufacturers.

- Preface -

This book is presented according to Northern Pacific's operating divisions as of January 1955. The middle of this decade was chosen to represent the diverse motive power operating during that interesting period. There were still quite a number of early steam locomotives in active service, but the era of the diesel was already making inroads in their ranks.

Most of Northern Pacific's modern steam locomotives, the A and Z Classes, remained in service, however, many of the passenger engines had been relegated to spend their remaining years in freight service.

During 1955, there was a surprising number of steam locomotives in active service considering that all had been retired by 1958, three years hence. The reason for this was the fact that scores of modern diesel switch engines, road switchers and F9 road locomotives were purchased between 1955 and 1960. A rather severe recession between 1956 and 1958, following the Korean Conflict, also added to the rather early demise of the steam locomotive.

It is impossible to gather color slides, all photographed on our roster date, January 1, 1955. Due to this fact some photos illustrate a particular locomotive on a different division than where it was assigned in 1955. For example, many of the smaller steam engines had been moved east after 1955, but they are located in the book with their 1955 assignment.

However, every effort has been made to illustrate each locomotive with its 1955 division assignment.

The seven division rosters in this book precede each division chapter. There are also several locomotive model rosters located throughout the book, inserted within the division the majority of that locomotive type are assigned. For example, during 1955, all of the passenger diesel locomotives were assigned to the St. Paul Division. The passenger F3, F5 and F7 roster is on pages 36 and 37 within the St. Paul Division's chapter. At the rear of the book is a steam locomotive roster as of January 1955, our roster date. There is also a couple of unique pages for the NP modeler. Facing pages 76 and 77 illustrate each type of EMD F cab-unit represented on the NP - FT, F-3, F-5, F-7 and F-9.

Northern Pacific Color Pictorial - Volume 2, features 1965 Division Locomotive Assignments, after all of the first generation diesels had been delivered, but before any second generation locomotives had been purchased.

Northern Pacific Color Pictorial - Volume 3, features 1969 Division Locomotive Assignments, illustrating all of the diesels, both first and second generation, on the roster prior to the BN merger. This volume also features the progression of Northern Pacific diesel locomotive painting via color photographs.

Northern Pacific's ten A-5 Class 4-8-4s, 2680-2689, were built under the authorization of the War Production Board for freight service by the Baldwin Locomotive Works between May and July 1943, during WWII. After the War these machines were relegated to passenger as well as freight service. In January 1955, our roster date, a pair of A-5s, 2681 and 2687, were assigned to passenger service on the Rocky Mountain Division. However, during the summer of 1954, Northern #2687 was working freight out of Parkwater, Washington. *Gayle Christen*

Northern Pacific Locomotive Assignment
Lake Superior Division
- January 1955 -

Locomotive No.	Class / Type		Service	Notes
100	DE	EMC NW	Switcher	Brainerd
710	DE	Alco S-2	Switcher	Duluth
713-717	DE	Alco S-4	Switcher	Duluth
1040	L-9	0-6-0	Switcher	Brainerd
1043	L-9	0-6-0	Switcher	Duluth
1051	L-9	0-6-0	Switcher	Cloquet
1058	L-9	0-6-0	Switcher	Duluth
1061	L-9	0-6-0	Switcher	Brainerd
1063	L-9	0-6-0	Switcher	Duluth
1065	L-9	0-6-0	Switcher	Stored awaiting disposition
1071, 1077, 1112-1114	L-9	0-6-0	Switcher	Duluth
1115, 1119	L-9	0-6-0	Switcher	Stored awaiting disposition
1120	L-9	0-6-0	Switcher	Duluth
1163-1164	L-10	0-6-0	Switcher	Duluth
1165	L-10	0-6-0	Switcher	Shop - Duluth Roundhouse
1166-1167	L-10	0-6-0	Switcher	Shop - Brainerd
1169	L-10	0-6-0	Switcher	Duluth
1175	G-2	0-8-0	Switcher	Shop - Brainerd
1177-1179	G-2	0-8-0	Switcher	Duluth
1182	G-2	0-8-0	Switcher	Awaiting shop time - Brainerd
1183	G-2	0-8-0	Switcher	Duluth
1506, 1535, 1541, 1577, 1588, 1605, 1609, 1632, 1647, 1657, 1659	W	2-8-2	Freight	
1681, 1683, 1686	W-1	2-8-2	Freight	
1707	W-3	2-8-2	Freight	
1734	W-3	2-8-2	Freight	Stored - Duluth
1740	W-3	2-8-2	Freight	Stored awaiting disposition
1749	W-3	2-8-2	Freight	
1758	W-3	2-8-2	Freight	Stored - Duluth
1764, 1768, 1790, 1805	W-3	2-8-2	Freight	
1807	W-3	2-8-2	Freight	Stored - Duluth
1819, 1827, 1832	W-3	2-8-2	Freight	
1837, 1839, 1841, 1845, 1846, 1849	W-5	2-8-2	Freight	
1852	W-5	2-8-2	Freight	Shop - Brainerd
1854, 1857, 1859	W-5	2-8-2	Freight	
2151	Q-3	4-6-2	Passenger	
2200, 2202	Q-4	4-6-2	Passenger	Stored - Duluth
2246, 2253, 2257	Q-6	4-6-2	Passenger	
2321, 2386	T	2-6-2	Freight	
2413	T	2-6-2	Freight	Stored awaiting disposition
2419	T	2-6-2	Switcher	Duluth
2424	T	2-6-2	Switcher	Bemidji
2430	T	2-6-2	Switcher	Awaiting shop time - Brainerd
2434, 2446	T	2-6-2	Freight	
2463, 2467	T-1	2-6-2	Switcher	Duluth

Northern Pacific Railway
- Lake Superior Division -

Ashland, WI. to Staples, MN. (Main Line) . . . . 206.65 mi.
Duluth Area Trackage (Main Line) . . . . 8.72 mi.
Duluth Union Depot Line (Main Line) . . . . 0.32 mi.
Duluth Short Line - White Bear Lake to Duluth, MN. (Main Line) . . . . 141.06 mi.
West Duluth Junction, MN. to Superior, WI. (West Superior Branch) . . . . 3.76 mi.
West Duluth Junction to New Duluth, MN. (Branch Line) . . . . 6.55 mi.
Carlton to Cloquet, MN. (Cloquet Branch) . . . . 6.79 mi.
Deerwood to Trommald and Riverton, MN. (Cuyuna Branch) . . . . 21.23 mi.
Brainerd to International Falls, MN. (International Falls Branch) . . . . 201.13 mi.
Funkley to Kelliher, MN. (Bullhead Lake Branch) . . . . 11.11 mi.

Lake Superior Division - Total Mileage . . . . 356.43 Main Lines - 250.89 Branch Lines

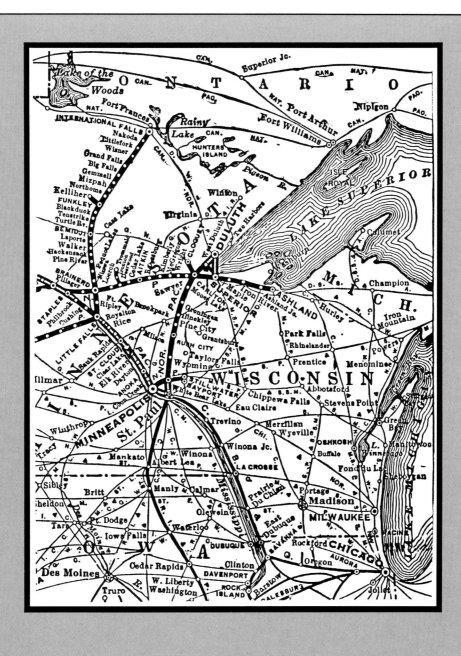

The United States Railway Administration (USRA) designed several locomotive wheel arrangements as standard during World War I. While many of these USRA designed locomotives were common in other parts of the country they were rather rare in the far West. However, the Northern Pacific did acquire four USRA 0-8-0's in 1919 (NP Class G-1), followed by twenty Alco built Class G-2 0-8-0's, 1174-1193, after the War during 1920. The 1178, one of a half-dozen Class G-2's assigned to the Lake Superior Division, is switching at West Duluth in sub-zero weather. *Wayne C. Olsen*

During January 1955, G-2 #1175 was in the shop at Brainerd, Minnesota, but by August 23rd the hefty USRA designed 0-8-0 switcher has been returned to local service working in the Duluth area. *Lou Schmitz*

Within a few years the many large coaling and steam watering stations along the NP system would become obsolete due to the arrival of the internal combustion diesel locomotive. However, in the mid-1950's, these intrusive structures were very active on the railroad scene as we see at Duluth, where class L-9 0-6-0 #1051 has just been serviced and passenger Class Q-6 4-6-2 #2246 awaits its turn. *Wayne C. Olsen*

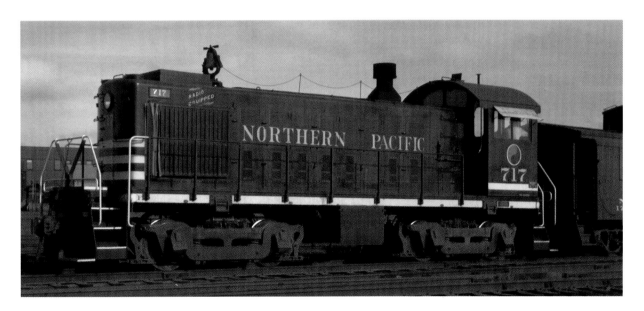

The Northern Pacific purchased a total of twelve Alco 1,000 horsepower S-4 switchers during the early 1950's. The 713-716 were acquired during October and November 1951. These were followed by 717-719 in May 1953 and finally 720-724 in December of that same year. Five Alco S-4s, including the 717, worked most their entire careers in the Duluth area, and by late 1957, all twelve S-4s called that northeastern Minnesota city home. *Robert Anderson*

Class L-9 #1114, one of twenty-one 0-6-0 switchers assigned to the Lake Superior Division in January 1955, switches a cut of cars at the 20th Avenue team track in the shadow of Soo Line's coal dock. The engineer of the little switcher is perched in a rather interesting and precarious position. *Wayne C. Olsen*

The 1051, a little L-9 Class 0-6-0, smokes it up as it works Cloquet, Minnesota, at the end of the 6.79 mile branch which stretches northwest from the main line at Carlton to Cloquet. *Ed Spitzer*

The three major classes of steam switchers assigned to the Lake Superior Division during January 1955 are represented on this page. Above, class L-9 #1112 is steamed up with a full tender of coal and ready for service at Duluth. *Lou Schmitz*

Right: One of NP's ten class L-10 0-6-0 switchers, 1160-1169, all assigned to the Lake Superior Division, is working the yard at Duluth. This class was built by Schenectady for the NP in 1912, and all were still in active service during the mid-1950's. The unique headlight jacket sets Northern Pacific's switchers apart from the thousands of 0-6-0s built for other American railroads during the early 1900's. *Robert Bruneau*

Northern Pacific's G-1 and G-2 Class 0-8-0 switchers were scattered throughout the entire system, and the Lake Superior Division was assigned a half-dozen G-2's in January 1955. The firemen working the G class switchers were assisted with tender mounted coal pushers. The 1178, a G-2, is assigned to heavy switching duties at Duluth on September 30, 1957. *Lou Schmitz*

Class W-3 2-8-2 Mikado #1819 is assigned the chore of switching ore loads on Northern Pacific's ore dock at Superior in August 1957. Over on Great Northern's ore docks EMD SD7s have already replaced steam and NP's W's won't be here much longer either, even though there were many more miles in most of these veterans. *Wayne C. Olsen*

Northern Pacific's twenty-five class W-5 locomotives, 1835-1859, were the railroad's largest and best 2-8-2 Mikados. "Mike" #1839 proudly displays the multitude of air pumps decorating its smokebox front, while the 1846, with an auxiliary tender, doubles-over a cut of cars at Duluth on April 9, 1954. *Left: Lou Schmitz*
Below: Dr. A. G. Chione

On August 10, 1957, freight Extra-1506, with a pair of W class 2-8-2s, one on the head end and another shoving, slowly work tonnage up the grade out of Duluth's Rices Point Yard. The 1647 is locking knuckles with caboose #1777 as the train passes DM&IR Junction. The pushers usually worked all the way to Superior and sometimes as far west as Carlton.
Wayne C. Olsen and Russ Porter

Northern Pacific's 2-8-2's were the steam equivalent of the GP9 road switcher from the early part of the 20th Century until replaced by hoards of GP9s during the mid-1950s. In January 1955, W-3 #1733 was assigned to helper service on the Rocky Mountain Division, but by August 1957, the 2-8-2 was working freight in the Duluth area. Racing along with local freights to realign turnouts was part of NP's health and exercise program for head brakemen. *Wayne C. Olsen*

In January 1955, W-5 #1852 was in the shop at Brainerd, but within a couple of months the sturdy "Mike" was back earning its keep in helper service on a freight extra near 19th Avenue-West in Duluth. *Wayne C. Olsen*

A freshly shopped class W-5 2-8-2 #1858, awaits a call on the ready track at Duluth. It has just been reassigned to the Lake Superior Division after visiting the Helena Roundhouse on the Rocky Mountain Division in January 1955. *Wayne C. Olsen*

Due to the temporary failure of the Duluth Union Depot & Transfer Co.'s diesel switching locomotive, Northern Pacific T Class 2-6-2 #2419 was leased. Above, NP 2419 has GN 181, one of Great Northern's unique EMD NW-3s assigned to their Duluth - Grand Forks passenger trains #35-36, in tow. Below, NP 2419, as DUD&T Co.'s switcher, is about to wye GN's five-car train set for #19-24, the St. Paul - Duluth *Gopher/Badger.* *Two photos - Wayne C. Olsen*

Shortly after the turn-of-the-century the Northern Pacific invested in a total of 150 Class T 2-6-2 locomotives, a wheel arrangement originally introduced by the Burlington Route, in which NP owns one half interest. Eighteen of these Prairie type engines were later modified into Class T-1 locomotives, 2450-2467. Class T-1 #2463, above, is switching 40-foot grain box cars at a Superior, Wisconsin elevator in September 1957. *Wayne C. Olsen*

Northern Pacific's W Class 2-8-2s were truly multi-purpose locomotives with solid steel pilots flanked with footboards for heavy switching service. The white-tired #1657 received yellow grab irons in 1955, as did most diesel switchers. The "Mike" was photographed at White Bear Lake , Minnesota on October 13, 1956. *Robert Bruneau*

A well manicured Pacific type locomotive sits at Duluth's Rices Point roundhouse ready track beside a Milwaukee Road EMD F-7 diesel freight set awaiting an assignment. The Q-6 Class was the zenith of Northern Pacific's stable of passenger 4-6-2s. The freshly serviced 2246, along with a Class W-3 2-8-2, will be called for a more mundane task today, as the proud Pacific will be called to work as a freight helper. *Wayne C. Olsen*

One month later, in September 1957, passenger #2246 is once again assigned to a different type of task. This time the 4-6-2 is temporary assigned on the Ledgerwood car to correct flat wheels on a W-3 Class locomotive. *Wayne C. Olsen*

Each Fall, during the mid and late 1950s, Class A-4 4-8-4 #2676 was moved from storage at St. Paul to Superior's Hill Avenue Yard to be used as a stationary steaming plant. The steam would be pumped into the iron ore cars to thaw out frozen ore arriving from the Cuyuna Iron Range. Several other iron haulers in the area provided similar services.
Two photos - Wayne C. Olsen

How shippers enjoy a broadcast without hearing it!

Conductor to engineer: "All black!" (no hot boxes)

If you ship freight, you'll like Northern Pacific's exciting new "radio program"—even though you can't hear it! We're talking about "broadcasts" between the locomotive and caboose of NP freight trains in the Cascade Mountains . . . via new two-way VHF radio telephone equipment. Why there? Because up in that lofty land of heavy weather, we can greatly expedite movement of your freight by keeping all crewmen constantly in touch with each other . . . even though they may be a mile apart. Keep tuned for further details . . .

Engineer to conductor: "OK, we're highballing!"

Our new "end to end" radio communication also means *safer* handling of your freight. In case of trouble—a hot box or sticking brakes—the engineer is told *instantly.* Northern Pacific is taking many other important steps to give you better shipping along the Main Street of the Northwest. We're buying new diesel power, building new freight cars, improving our right-of-way, and streamlining our loading-and-unloading procedures. Call on us next time you have a really *tough* shipping problem—offices located in principal cities.

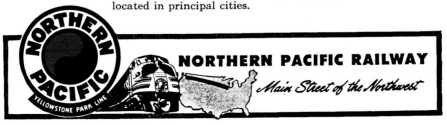

NORTHERN PACIFIC RAILWAY
Main Street of the Northwest

Northern Pacific Locomotive Assignment
Saint Paul Division
- January 1955 -

Locomotive No.	Class / Type		Service	Notes
24	Y-1	2-8-0	Switcher	St. Paul
27	Y-1	2-8-0	Switcher	Staples
34	Y	2-8-0	Switcher	Minneapolis
101	DE	EMC NW-2	Switcher	St. Paul
102-103	DE	EMC NW-2	Switcher	Minneapolis
104-105	DE	EMD NW-2	Switcher	St. Paul
106	DE	EMD NW-2	Switcher	St. Paul-Stillwater
107-110	DE	EMD SW-7	Switcher	Minneapolis
111	DE	EMD SW-7	Switcher	St. Paul
112-114	DE	EMD SW-7	Switcher	Minneapolis
117	DE	EMD SW-9	Switcher	Staples
118	DE	EMD SW-9	Switcher	St. Paul
550-551	DE	EMD GP7	Passenger	
559	DE	EMD GP7	Freight/Transfer	
803	DE	Alco RS-1	Switcher	Staples
856	DE	Alco RS-3	Switcher	Staples
1062	L-9	0-6-0	Switcher	Stillwater
1088	L-9	0-6-0	Switcher	St. Paul
1160	L-10	0-6-0	Switcher	Stillwater
1161-1162	L-10	0-6-0	Switcher	Minneapolis
1168	L-10	0-6-0	Switcher	East Grand Forks
1170, 1172	G-1	0-8-0	Switcher	Minneapolis
1173	G-1	0-8-0	Switcher	Staples
1181	G-2	0-8-0	Switcher	Minneapolis
1184	G-2	0-8-0	Switcher	Staples
1514	W	2-8-2	Switcher	Staples
1519	W	2-8-2	Freight	
1545	W	2-8-2	Switcher	Minneapolis
1550-1551	W	2-8-2	Freight	
1552	W	2-8-2	Freight	Shop - Staples Roundhouse
1554	W	2-8-2	Switcher	Minneapolis
1558, 1561, 1565, 1574	W	2-8-2	Freight	
1576	W	2-8-2	Switcher	Minneapolis
1606	W	2-8-2	Freight	
1642	W	2-8-2	Switcher	Minneapolis
1646, 1649	W	2-8-2	Freight	
1662-1664, 1668	W-1	2-8-2	Freight	
1669	W-1	2-8-2	Freight	Shop - Brainerd
1673, 1684-1685	W-1	2-8-2	Freight	
1737	W-3	2-8-2	Freight	Stored awaiting disposition
1793, 1798, 1806, 1817	W-3	2-8-2	Freight	
1825	W-3	2-8-2	Freight	Stored awaiting disposition
1836	W-5	2-8-2	Freight	
1847	W-5	2-8-2	Freight	Stored awaiting disposition
2150	Q-3	4-6-2	Passenger	Stored - Staples
2153	Q-3	4-6-2	Passenger	Stored - Dilworth
2183	Q-4	4-6-2	Passenger	

Northern Pacific Locomotive Assignment
Saint Paul Division (Continued)
- January 1955 -

Locomotive No.	Class / Type		Service	Notes
2305	T	2-6-2	Switcher	East Grand Forks
2315	T	2-6-2	Switcher	Shop - Staples Roundhouse
2385	T	2-6-2	Switcher	East Grand Forks
2407	T	2-6-2	Freight	
2416	T	2-6-2	Switcher	East Grand Forks
2450, 2456	T-1	2-6-2	Switcher	St. Cloud-Minneapolis
2457	T-1	2-6-2	Switcher	Shop - Northtown Roundhouse
2465-2466	T-1	2-6-2	Freight	
2663	A-3	4-8-4	Freight	
2666	A-3	4-8-4	Freight	Stored awaiting disposition
2673, 2676	A-4	4-8-4	Passenger	Stored - St. Paul
2677	A-4	4-8-4	Passenger	
2680	A-5	4-8-4	Passenger	Stored - Northtown
2682	A-5	4-8-4	Passenger	Stored - Jamestown
2683	A-5	4-8-4	Passenger	Stored - Northtown
2684	A-5	4-8-4	Passenger	Stored - St. Paul
2685-2686	A-5	4-8-4	Freight	
2688	A-5	4-8-4	Freight	Livingston Shop
6500A-B-C	DE	EMD F3A/F3B/F7A	Passenger	
6501A-B-C	DE	EMD F3A/F3B/F7A	Passenger	
6502A-B-C	DE	EMD F3A/F3B/F7A	Passenger	
6503A-B-C	DE	EMD F3A/F3B/F5A	Passenger	
6504A-B-C	DE	EMD F3A/F3B/F5A	Passenger	
6505A-B-C	DE	EMD F3A/F3B/F5A	Passenger	
6506A-B-C	DE	EMD F3A/F3B/F5A	Passenger	
6507A-B-C	DE	EMD F7A/F3B/F7A	Passenger	
6508A-B-C	DE	EMD F7A/F3B/F7A	Passenger	
6509A-B-C	DE	EMD F7A/F3B/F7A	Passenger	
6510A-B-C	DE	EMD F7A/F7B/F7A	Passenger	
6511A-B-C	DE	EMD F7A/F7B/F7A	Passenger	
6512A-B-C	DE	EMD F7A/F7B/F7A	Passenger	
6513A-B-C	DE	EMD F7A/F7B/F7A	Passenger	
6550B	DE	EMD F7B	Passenger	(Extra B-unit)
6600A-6601A	DE	EMD FP7	Passenger	
6700A-B-C	DE	EMD F9A/F9B/F9A	Passenger	

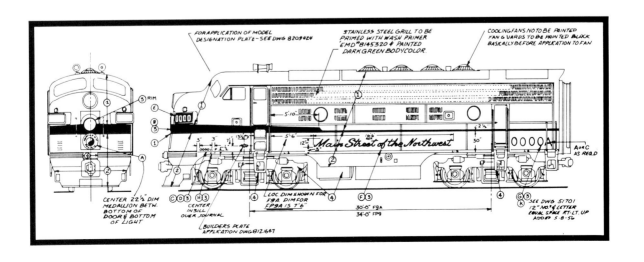

Northern Pacific Railway
- Saint Paul Division -

Saint Paul to Staples, MN. (Main Line)	146.80 mi.
Staples to Dilworth, MN. (Main Line)	103.63 mi.
Duluth Short Line - St. Paul to White Bear Lake, MN. (Main Line)	11.04 mi.
Soo Line connections at Trout Brook and Gloster, MN. (Main Line)	0.27 mi.
Little Falls to Brainerd, MN. (Main Line)	30.58 mi.
Saint Paul Union Depot terminals (Main Line)	0.57 mi.
Mulberry Street Branch in Minneapolis, MN.	0.85 mi.
Minneapolis to White Bear Lake, MN. (Minneapolis Branch)	13.74 mi.
White Bear Lake to Stillwater, MN. (Stillwater Branch)	12.73 mi.
Little Falls to Morris, MN. (Little Falls and Dakota Branch)	87.04 mi.
Wadena, MN. to Oakes, N.D. (Fergus Falls Branch)	150.80 mi.
Fairview Junction, MN. to Great Bend, N.D. (Fairview Branch)	8.82 mi.
Manitoba Junction, MN. to Pembina, N.D. (Red River Branch)	190.39 mi.
Tiden Junction to Carthage Junction, MN. (Red Lake Falls Branch)	43.88 mi.
Key West to Sherack, MN. (Sherack Branch)	6.13 mi.
Midland Ry. of Manitoba in Winnipeg, Manitoba, Canada (Joint Ownership)	5.66 mi.
Trackage rights (Main Line)	11.84 mi.
Trackage rights (Branch Line)	83.34 mi.

Saint Paul Division - Total Mileage . . . . 307.69 Main Lines - 603.38 Branch Lines

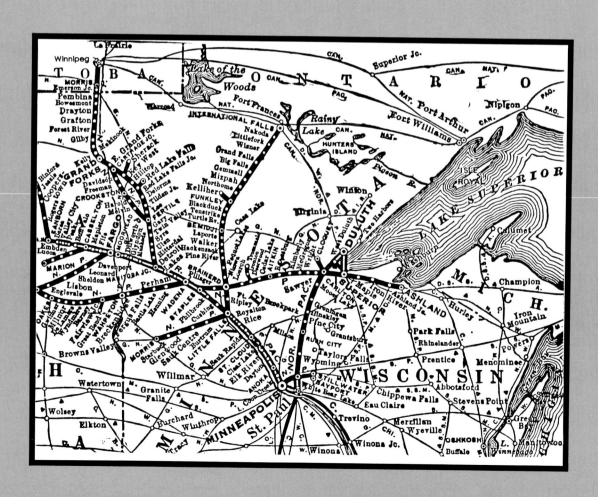

One of four Class W, light 2-8-2s assigned to Minneapolis, #1554, is working the west end of Northtown Yard on a slightly overcast October 14, 1956 morning. During the mid-1950s, the Minneapolis area was assigned a wide variety of switch engines which included everything from an old Y Class 2-8-0 and little 0-6-0s to modern EMD SW-7 diesel switchers. *Robert Bruneau*

NP SW-7 #108, a 1949 product of EMD, is approaching Northtown on a local switch run from Fridley and Coon Rapids. Even though it's June the switcher still wears its extended vision side window for winter operation on the engineer's side of the cab. The "open door" type of air conditioning is in operation on this warm early summer Minnesota day. *Ross Hammond*

After extensive evaluations with EMC NW #100 beginning in late December 1938, the Northern Pacific purchased three 1000-horsepower NW-2 switchers, NP 101-103, from EMC in March 1940, for the Twin Cities Area. NP #101 retained its St. Paul assignment until May 1955, when it was reassigned to Brainerd on the Lake Superior Division. Two years later it was sent to Seattle where it worked until its retirement at Auburn in 1969. The 101 was the only NP NW-2 scrapped prior to the BN merger. *Dave Ingles photo - Al Chione collection*

A winter scene taken near the same area displays the stark contrast in Minnesota seasons. Class W #1574 is departing Northtown with a local freight in -15 degree F. weather in December 1953. The display of steam and smoke piercing the cold air make for an awesome spectacle. *Russ Porter*

Another class W 2-8-2, NP 1545, is assigned as a Minneapolis switcher in this May 30, 1952 photo. Note the unique double spouted water tank between the tracks. Also notice the large number of 40-foot box cars in the yard tracks. Many of these were assigned to grain loading, and replaced years later by jumbo covered hoppers. *Russ Porter*

Due to the lack of engine number indicator boards on locomotive #1576, it must have been assigned to yard switching service for some time. The "Mike's" tender has just been replenished with coal and water at Minneapolis on October 14, 1956. *Robert Bruneau*

The Northern Pacific invested in 150 Class T 2-6-2 Prairie Type locomotives, 2300-2449, all built by Brooks in 1906 and 1907. Eighteen were later modified and reclassified as T-1, and renumbered as 2450-2467. Several of these rebuilt T-1's were assigned to freight and switching service on the Saint Paul Division. NP #2456, left, is assigned to local service between St. Cloud and Minneapolis, while #2457 below, performs yard chores at Northtown in July 1957. *Left: Robert Bruneau*
Below: Russ Porter

During January 1955, the St. Paul Division was allocated a single Alco RS-1, #803, and the 1000-horsepower road switcher was assigned to switching service at Staples, Minnesota. This veteran of August 1945, was originally numbered 1st 158. *Ed Kanak photo - Ed Fulcomer collection*

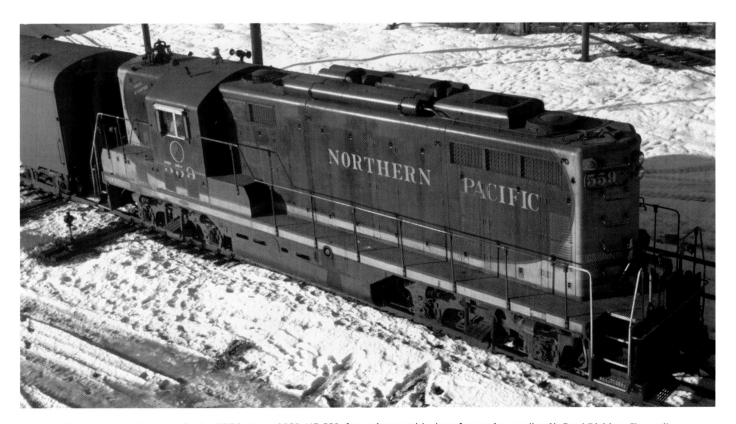

The railroad ordered a single GP7 in June 1952, NP 559, for assignment to transfer service on the St. Paul Division. The unit was purchased with extra large fuel tanks necessitating the four air-reservoir tanks to be roof mounted. This photo affords an excellent view of the roof arrangement. *Jerry Quinn*

There were a dozen big modern 4-8-4's assigned to the St. Paul Division in January 1955. Some were assigned to freight service, some were assigned to passenger service and a few were stored serviceable due to the normal January seasonal downturn in business. However, on a cold, clear January 20, 1946, we find one of these big Northern's, a class A-3, #2663 in passenger service, being serviced at Livingston, Montana.   *E.T. Harley*

In January 1955, the 2682, a St. Paul Division assigned passenger class A-5 Northern, was stored serviceable at Jamestown, North Dakota, but by August 21st, the big 4-8-4 with its huge tender, had returned to active service and was awaiting a call to duty.   *Lou Schmitz*

Another Northern which was stored serviceable in January 1955 was A-4 #2673. By September 5, 1956, the big 4-8-4 was working a westbound freight, #605, through Tusler, Montana in the Yellowstone Valley, just east of Miles City, with 132 cars in tow. Their solid steel pilots with folding couplers made the A-4's appear even more massive. *Warren McGee*

During the post-War year of 1946, three Class A-3 4-8-4s were assigned to passenger service on the Idaho Division while the other five were on the Rocky Mountain Division. A-3 #2663 is on one section of the *North Coast Limited* while making its station stop at Butte, Montana on January 20th. By the early 1950s, all eight A-3s were assigned to the St. Paul Division, but by January 1955, only the 2663 remained in active service on the division. *E.T. Harley*

Northern #2683 was one of ten Class A-5 4-8-4s built by the Baldwin Locomotive Works during the summer of 1943. Delivered during WWII, these were the last non-articulated steam locomotives purchased by the Northern Pacific. Their tenders rode on huge articulated Commonwealth "centipede" trucks in a 4-10-0 wheel arrangement. They were capable of carrying 54,000 pounds of coal and 25,000 gallons of water, rendering the locomotives a very long operating range. Most of NP's 4-8-4s had many serviceable miles remaining when they were retired during the mid and late 1950s. *R.R. Wallin collection*

As of January 1955, our roster date, Class A-4 #2676, which had been assigned to passenger service, was stored at St. Paul. By September 4, 1956 the classy Northern was working freight through Frazee, Minnesota with Time Freight #605 consisting of 130 cars/3,905 tons. The fast freight is heading for Laurel, Montana where its schedule terminated. *Warren McGee*

On September 6, 1955, Class A-5 Northern #2683 was at the Staples, Minnesota coal dock. Today, Staples is the site of a unique fueling station for successor Burlington Northern, as it is the location of BN's sole LNG (Liquified Natural Gas) refueling depot. *Robert Bruneau*

A pair of refueled Class W-1 2-8-2s stand on the ready track awaiting a call for local freight service, while in the background, a freight extra powered by relatively new F-units approaches. The mid-1940s through the late 1950s, was the general transitional period from steam to diesel on most major American and Canadian railroads. *Al Chione collection*

Northern Pacific's Class A-5 Northern's were purchased for fast freight service in 1943. Originally six of the ten locomotives were assigned between Northtown (Minneapolis) and Mandan, North Dakota, a distance of 437 miles, while the other four were assigned between Glendive and Laurel, Montana, 241 miles. On September 9, 1955, the class engine, #2680, was slowly moving from Mandan's roundhouse to the yard to couple onto its eastbound manifest. *Robert Bruneau*

As of January 1955, there were fifteen 3-unit passenger locomotives, plus an extra booster unit, assigned to the St. Paul Division for transcontinental passenger service. NP 6500 through 6502 consisted of the combination of an F3A/F3B/F7A set, while 6503 through 6506 consisted of an F3A/F3B/F5A set, 6507 through 6509 consisted of an F7A/F3B/F7A set, 6510 through 6513 consisted of solid F7A-B-A sets and finally 6700A-B-C was the first F9 locomotive set already on line. In September 1956, #6501A, an F3A/F3B/F7A set leads the Vista-Dome *North Coast Limited* near Miles City, Montana. The locomotive grillwork is the main spotting feature in this photo. *Ed Gerlits*

NP's first seven 3-unit passenger locomotives, 6500-6506, were delivered in 1947, consisting of F3 A-B-B sets. Turning this configuration at each end was determined to present a problem which was resolved by swapping newer F3As (F5As on the NP) and F7As. (See the rearranged roster on page 36.) Presented here is the F3 and F5 cab units for locomotive #6501. The F3As were delivered with three portholes and no air filter louvers. This center panel was rearranged by eliminating the center porthole and adding four air-filter louvers in the center side panel.
Center: Fred Scott
Lower: Dave Ingles photo -John Shine Coll.

Northern Pacific F3, F5 & F7 Passenger Locomotives
- January 1955 -

Previous Road No.	Road No. 1955	Model	Date Built	EMD Const. No.	Notes & Disposition
	6500A	EMD F3A	1/47	3773	Traded-in to GE for U25C 4/64.
6500C (1st)	6500B (2nd)	EMD F3B	1/47	3788	[From 1st 6500C - 10/49] Renumbered 6509B 9/49 (See below)
	6500C (2nd)	EMD F7A	9/49	8731	Wrecked Cheney, WA 8/55, reblt. as F9A, 3/56, re# 6703C 6/65.
	6501A	EMD F3A	1/47	3774	Traded-in to GE for U28C 7/66.
	6501B	EMD F3B	1/47	3789	Traded-in to EMD for SD45 7/66.
	6501C (2nd)	EMD F7A	4/49	7150	Renumbered 6507B 4/49 (See below)
	6502A	EMD F3A	1/47	3775	Assigned to Amtrak 5/71, sold to Nap. Bros. Iron & Metal 11/73.
	6502B	EMD F3B	1/47	3791	Traded-in to GE for U25C 9/65.
	6502C (2nd)	EMD F7A	4/49	7151	To BN 9764, sold to Amtrak as #100 8/72, retired Seattle 10/75.
	6503A	EMD F3A	1/47	3776	Assigned to Amrtak 5/71, sold to Precision National Corp., 4/74.
6503C (1st)	6503B (2nd)	EMD F3B	1/47	3794	[From 1st 6503C - 11/48] Traded-in to GE for U25C 9/65.
	6503C (2nd)	EMD F5A	10/48	6652	Traded-in to GE for U25C 9/65.
	6504A	EMD F3A	1/47	3777	Traded-in to GE for U25C 9/65.
6504C (1st)	6504B (2nd)	EMD F3B	1/47	3796	[From 1st 6504C - 11/48] Traded-in to GE for U28C 7/66.
	6504C (2nd)	EMD F5A	10/48	6653	Traded-in to EMD for SD45 2/67.
	6505A	EMD F3A	1/47	3778	Traded-in to EMD for SD45 8/66.
6505C (1st)	6505B (2nd)	EMD F3B	1/47	3873	[From 1st 6505C - 11/48] Traded-in to GE for U25C 9/65.
	6505C (2nd)	EMD F5A	10/48	6654	Traded-in to EMD for SD45 3/67.
	6506A	EMD F3A	4/47	4787	Traded-in to EMD for SD45 7/66.
6506C (1st)	6506B (2nd)	EMD F3B	4/47	4789	[From 1st 6506C - 10/48] Traded-in to GE for U25C 5/64.
	6506C (2nd)	EMD F5A	10/48	6655	Traded-in to GE for U33C 7/69.
	6507A	EMD F7A	4/49	7146	Traded-in to EMD for SD45 4/70 by BN.
6501C (1st)	6507B	EMD F3B	1/47	3790	[From 1st 6501C - 4/49] To BN 9763, assigned to Amtrak 5/71, sold to Precision National Corp., 9/74.
	6507C	EMD F7A	4/49	7147	To BN 9772, sold to Precision National Corp., 4/74.
	6508A	EMD F7A	4/49	7148	Wrecked at Granite, ID. 3/62, Dismantled 5/62.
6502C (1st)	6508B	EMD F3B	1/47	3792	[From 1st 6502C - 4/49] Traded-in to GE for U25C 9/65.
	6508C	EMD F7A	4/49	7149	To BN 9774, sold to Amtrak as #102 8/72, traded-in to EMD 1/76
	6509A	EMD F7A	9/49	8732	To BN 9776, sold to Amrtak as #101 8/72, re#102, traded-in to EMD 1/76.
6500B (1st)	6509B	EMD F3B	1/47	3787	[From 1st 6500B - 9/49] To BN 9765, assigned to Amtrak 5/71, sold to Alter Co. 12/72.
	6509C	EMD F7A	9/49	8733	To BN 9778, sold to Amtrak as #103 8/72, retired Minneapolis '75
	6510A	EMD F7A	9/49	8734	Traded-in to EMD for SD45 3/67.
	6510B	EMD F7B	9/49	8740	To BN 9767, sold to Amtrak as #152 8/72, traded-in to EMD 1/76
	6510C	EMD F7A	9/49	8735	Traded-in to GE for U28C 7/66.
	6511A	EMD F7A	9/49	8736	To BN 9780, sold to Amtrak as #104 8/72, retired Minn. 11/73.
	6511B	EMD F7B	9/49	8741	To BN 9769, sold to Amtrak as #153 8/72, traded-in to EMD 1/76
	6511C	EMD F7A	9/49	8737	To BN 9782, sold to Amtrak as #105 8/72, traded-in to EMD 1/76
	6512A	EMD F7A	9/49	8738	To BN 9784, sold to Amtrak as #106 8/72, traded-in to EMD 1/76
	6512B	EMD F7B	9/49	8742	Wrecked at Granite, ID. 3/62, dismantled 8/62.
	6512C	EMD F7A	9/49	8739	To BN 9786, sold to Precision Engineering Co., 11/70.
	6513A	EMD F7A	2/50	10855	To BN 9788, sold to Amtrak as #107 8/72, traded-in to EMD 1/76
	6513B	EMD F7B	2/50	10857	To BN 9771, sold to Amtrak as #154 8/72, traded-in to EMD 1/76
	6513C	EMD F7A	2/50	10856	To BN 9790, re# (2nd) BN 724 9/76, sold to J. Simon & Sons '81.

Northern Pacific F3, F5, F7, & FP7 Passenger Locomotives
(Continued)
- January 1955 -

Previous Road No.	Road No. 1955	Model	Date Built	EMD Const. No.	Notes & Disposition
	6550B	EMD F7B	2/52	15683	[Purchased as an extra passenger unit] Traded-in to EMD for SD45 7/70 by BN.
6505B (1st) to 6017B (1st) to 6006B (2nd) to [6551B]		EMD F3B	1/47	3872	Originally 1st 6505B, converted to freight 1st 6017B 11/48 (see page 66), re# (2nd) 6006B 1/50, reconverted to passenger 6551B [12/59], to BN 9775, sold to Amtrak as #155 8/72, traded-in to EMD 1/76.
6506B (1st) to 6017C (1st) to 6006C (2nd) to [6552B]		EMD F3B	4/47	4788	Originally 1st 6506B, converted to freight 1st 6017C 11/48 (see page 66), re# (2nd) 6006C 1/50, reconverted to passenger 6552B [3/60], to BN 9777, sold to Amtrak as #156 8/72, traded-in to EMD 1/76.
6504B (1st) to 6016B (1st) to 5005C (2nd) to [6553]		EMD F3B	1/47	3795	Originally 1st 6504B, converted to freight 1st 6016B 11/48 (see page 66), re# (2nd) 6005C 1/50, reconverted to passenger 6553B [6/62], traded-in to EMD for SD45 5/67.

(Note - 6551B, 6552B and 6553B were added to this roster after January 1955, but are included here for completeness.)

	6600	EMD FP7	2/52	15681	To BN 9792; sold to Naporano Bros. Iron & Metal Co. 11/73.
	6601	EMD FP7	2/52	15682	To BN 9794; re# BN 726 (freight) 9/76; wrecked at Auburn, WA 2/80, scrapped by BN 9/80.
	6700A	EMD F9A	2/54	19056	To BN 9800; re# BN 766 (freight) 9/76; rebuilt to SPU 972567 12/81; rebuilt to F9A-2 (3rd) BN 1 10/90.
	6700B	EMD F9B	2/54	19058	To BN 9801; re# BN 767 (freight) 9/76; traded-in to GE for B30-7AB 8/82.
	6700C (1st)	EMD F9A	2/54	19057	Wrecked at Granite, ID 3/62, dismantled 5/62.

(Note - 6700A-B-C was the only F9 passenger set on the roster by Jan. 1955-Many more were to come. See NP Volume 2)

A pair of passenger F3As bask in the sun at Livingston, Montana. The 6504A is one of the original F3As built in January 1947 for the *North Coast Limited*. NP 2nd 6503C is a late model F3A (NP F5A), a cab-unit purchased in October 1948 to replace the 1st 6503C, an F3 booster-unit which became 2nd 6503B which, in turn, replaced B-unit 1st 6503B which was converted to freight 1st 6016C in November 1948. Follow all of that? *Matthew J. Herson*

The *North Coast Limited* is making its early morning station stop at Missoula in western Montana, the headquarters of the Rocky Mountain Division, on July 28, 1955. This mid-summer Vista-Dome streamliner is powered by 6504C-B-A an F5A/F3B/F3A locomotive combination. *Montague Powell*

Many changes, other than the center panel, have been perpetrated on the original F3A units. NP 6503A illustrates cab-unit additions consisting of grabs above the cab windows and on the right side behind the number boards, making it easier for window washing. A pair of wrecking lift rings have been added just above the buffer. New horns, a radio antenna, along with "Radio Equipped" stencils and a winterization hatch has been added to the rear roof fan, not to mention a new modern paint scheme. Even the lettering around the Monad has been changed from "Northern Pacific" to "Northern Pacific Railway". *Ed Fulcomer*

The modern two-tone green passenger scheme designed by Raymond Loewy was adopted for the NP in late 1953. In this June 1956 photo of the famous *North Coast Limited*, making its station stop in Fargo, the cars from the eighth back remain in the original scheme. *Fred Scott*

NP's Train #2, the *Mainstreeter*, is rushing past the depot at Hauser Junction, Idaho in June 1955, with 6509C-B-A. There are a few interesting items to notice in this photo. First, the 6509C still carries the now obsolete "Northern Pacific" Monad (a 1954 change), it still has its original air horns and the grab irons have not yet been added on the right front side of the cab. Radio equipment has not yet been added either. Notice also that the F3B has had its center porthole replaced with an air-filter louvre, standard on most of NP's passenger F3 booster units. *Alfred B. Butler*

The 6507A-B-C illustrates one of the three passenger locomotives, 6507-6509, made up of F7A/F3B/F7A combinations. The 6507A has just uncoupled from the passenger cars at St. Paul displaying the open doors at the bottom of the pilot accessing the steam lines for passenger operation. *Tom Smart*

Every Spring the mountains of south-central Montana are covered with a green mantle and wild flowers flourish, even between the rails, as the pride of Northern Pacific's passenger service, the Vista-Dome *North Coast Limited*, winds its way through this beautiful Western countryside. *John Shine collection*

Below: NP F7A #6511C has just led 6700A-B-C, NP's first passenger F9 set, into Livingston, Montana where the locomotives will be changed out. The first and last cars have been "Blue Flagged" and the motive power will soon be cut from the consist. *Harry L. Juday photo - Ed Fulcomer collection*

With a rather unusual motive power consist, just a pair of cab-units, 6513C and 6513A, the eastbound *North Coast Limited* makes its station stop at Billings, Montana during the summer of 1955. Perhaps the booster unit had been removed due to mechanical problems further west. Notice, the letters "A" and "C" have not yet been added the carbodies.
Jim Newell

Once again the 6513B is missing from the locomotive consist. This time spare F7B #6550 has been substituted for the "normal" B-unit on train #408, a Coast Pool Train from Seattle to Portland. *Matthew J. Herson - R.R. Wallin collection*

Northern Pacific's last passenger F7 locomotive set, #6513A-B-C, were delivered in
February 1950, and for awhile were operated separately as spare units. The 6513C
is at Seattle's King Street Station.
William J. Neill

While all of Northern Pacific's passenger
F3s, F5s, F7s and F9s were all equipped
with dynamic braking, only the F7s and F9s
had the extra fifth roof fan for dynamic
brake cooling. The F3s and F5s simply had
a pair of rectangular roof filters which
were out of sight from ground level. The
6506A illustrates the four typical high F3
roof fans with the steam boiler exhaust
vent pipe near the rear of the unit. During
the summer months the crews were glad
the steam boilers were in the rear of the
locomotives. The 6506A was photographed at St. Paul, where all of NP's passenger units were assigned until 1958,
when most road power was reassigned to
Livingston for maintenance.
Dave Ingles photo - R.R. Wallin collection

The Northern Pacific purchased a pair of EMD FP-7 units, 6600-6601, in early 1952, for use on passenger trains 11-12 between
St. Paul and International Falls, Minnesota and on trains 61 and 62 between St. Paul and Duluth. They replaced a pair of
passenger equipped GP-7 road switchers, #550 and 551. In-as-much as these new FP-7s would not be operated in the
mountainous region in the west, they were not equipped with dynamic brakes. The 6601 was photographed at St. Paul,
its home base during most of its career. *Tom Smart*

NP eventually acquired a roster of eight passenger F9 locomotives plus three spare F9B units. However, by 1955, there was only a single F9 locomotive set, 6700A-B-C, which entered service in March 1954. The F9s each produced 1,750 horsepower per unit for a total of 5,250 horsepower per three-unit locomotive. The distinguishing feature separating the F7s and F9s was that the F9s had an additional air-filter louvre just ahead of the front porthole. The 6700 is working one of the Coast Pool Trains between Seattle and Portland. *Ken Crist*

Summer and Winter - Livingston, Montana was the change out point for transcontinental passenger power for the Northern Pacific, both eastbound and westbound trains. Above, the F9 passenger set of 6700A-B-C is about to be replaced on the eastbound *North Coast Limited* with 6504C an EMD F5A, while in the cold of Winter, below, 6500C and 6510C are about to change places on eastbound Number 26. *Above: Matthew J. Herson - Below: Gil Hulin*

Northern Pacific Locomotive Assignment
Fargo Division
- January 1955 -

Locomotive No.	Class / Type		Service	Notes
21	Y-1	2-8-0	Switcher	Jamestown
26	Y-1	2-8-0	Switcher	Jamestown
603	DE	Alco S-1	Switcher	Fargo-Dilworth
700-703	DE	Alco S-2	Switcher	Fargo-Dilworth
800-802	DE	Alco RS-1	Freight	
850-852, 855	DE	Alco RS-3	Freight	
1213	Y-3	2-8-0	Switcher	Dilworth
1504, 1573	W	2-8-2	Freight	
1578, 1581	W	2-8-2	Switcher	Dilworth
1585	W	2-8-2	Freight	Stored - Dilworth
1595, 1597	W	2-8-2	Freight	
1613, 1623, 1651	W	2-8-2	Freight	Stored - Jamestown
1660	W-1	2-8-2	Freight	
1666	W-1	2-8-2	Freight	Shop - Dilworth Roundhouse
1687-1688	W-1	2-8-2	Freight	
1715, 1721, 1743	W-3	2-8-2	Freight	
1746, 1774	W-3	2-8-2	Freight	Stored - Jamestown
1822, 1833	W-3	2-8-2	Freight	
1916, 1918	W-2	2-8-2	Freight	
2160	Q-3	4-6-2	Freight	Mixed
2162	Q-3	4-6-2	Freight	
2164	Q-3	4-6-2	Freight	Stored - Jamestown
2180	Q-4	4-6-2	Freight	
2182, 2192	Q-4	4-6-2	Freight	Mixed
2220	Q-4	4-6-2	Freight	Stored - Mandan
2223	Q-4	4-6-2	Freight	Mixed
2454	T-1	2-6-2	Freight	
2455	T-1	2-6-2	Freight	Shop - Jamestown Roundhouse
2459-2460	T-1	2-6-2	Freight	

Northern Pacific Railway
- Fargo Division -

Dilworth, MN. to Jamestown, N.D. (Main Line) . . . . 99.68 mi.

Jamestown to Mandan, N.D. (Main Line) . . . . 106.46 mi.

Peak to Berea, N.D. - Low Line - (Main Line) . . . . 10.28 mi.

Fergus Falls Branch in Oakes, N.D. . . . . 0.28 mi.

Fargo to Streeter, N.D. (Fargo & Southwestern Branch) . . . . 148.51 mi.

Casselton to Marion, N.D. (Casselton Branch) . . . . 60.13 mi.

Sanborn to McHenry, N.D. (Cooperstown Branch) . . . . 62.88 mi.

Jamestown to LaMoure, N.D. (James River Branch) . . . . 48.51 mi.

Independence to Oakes, N.D. (Oakes Branch) . . . . 15.26 mi.

Jamestown to Leeds, N.D. (Devils Lake Branch) . . . . 108.24 mi.

Pingree to Wilton, N.D. (Wilton Branch) . . . . 92.81 mi.

Carrington to Turtle Lake, N.D. (Sykeston Branch) . . . . 85.02 mi.

Oberon to Esmond, N.D. (Oberon Branch) . . . . 28.08 mi.

McKenzie to Linton, N.D. (Linton Branch) . . . . 44.21 mi.

Mandan to Cannon Ball and Mott, N.D. (Mandan South Line) . . . . 128.00 mi.

Mandan to Killdeer, N.D. (Mandan North Line) . . . . 121.35 mi.

Truax Junction to Truax, N.D. (Truax Branch) . . . . 6.37 mi.

Other Trackage - Terminal and Joint Trackage . . . . 1.16 mi.

Fargo Division - Total Mileage . . . . 216.42 Main Lines - 950.87 Branch Lines

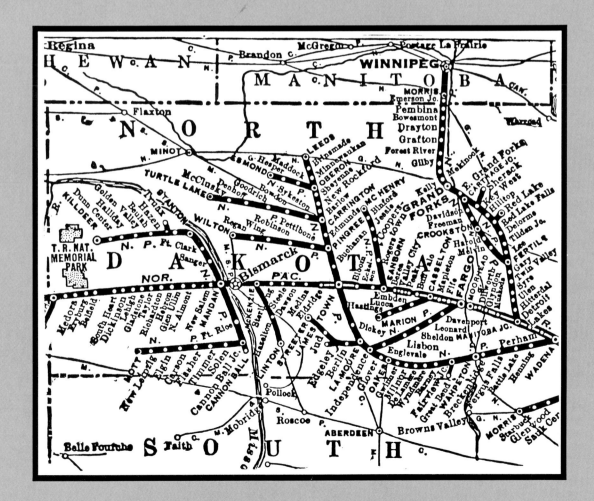

During January 1955, Class W-3 2-8-2 #1721 and #1833, below, were both assigned to freight service on the Fargo Division. However, by the summer of 1957, both "Mike's" had been reassigned to the Lake Superior Division. NP 1721 is working a drag freight at 63rd Avenue-West at West Duluth Junction in August 1957, while #1833 is arriving at Superior with a transfer run near the Winter Street crossing. *Two photos - Wayne C. Olsen*

The Northern Pacific purchased but one Alco non-turbocharged 660-horsepower S-1 in August 1945. Originally numbered 1st 131, the little Alco switcher was renumbered 603 at Fargo, ND in March 1950. The unique switcher was a resident of Fargo/Dilworth until January of 1958, when it was transferred to the Tacoma Division and leased to Seattle's King Street Station where it switched passenger and express cars. *James M. Adams*

The much more common type of Alco switcher on the NP was the 1000-horsepower S-2 model. The turbocharged six-cylinder diesel engine produced more tractive effort than NP's common steam powered 0-6-0 switchers or even their heavy USRA 0-8-0 types. Between March 1941 and December 1949, the NP purchased thirteen S-2s from Alco. The first eleven were originally numbered 1st 107-108, 113-118 and 150-152. In December 1949/January 1950, they were renumbered 700-710, while the last pair, 711 and 712, were purchased in December 1949. The 700, below, is at the Division Point of Dilworth, Minnesota, while #701 is working in local service at Moorhead, Minnesota. *Right: Douglas R. Martin Below: Ed Fulcomer collection*

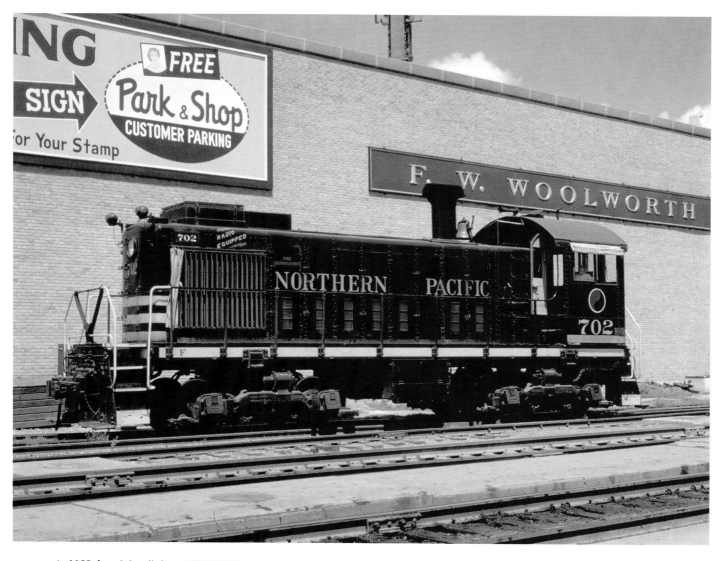

In 1955, four S-2 switchers, NP 700-703, were assigned to the Fargo/Moorhead/Dilworth area. They were augmented by a Y-3 Class 2-8-0 and a pair of Class W 2-8-2s for switching service at the Dilworth Yard. The 702, with Alco's classic Blunt trucks, unique only with their S-1 and S-2 switchers, is working at Fargo in the Red River Valley of southeastern North Dakota. For the modelers we present the opposite side of the same locomotive. *Above: Bob Gevaert - Ed Fulcomer collection Below: R.R. Wallin collection*

NP's Alco RS-1 turbocharged 1000-horsepower road switchers, 1st 155-158, were originally scattered throughout the system, however by 1955, three of the four RS-1s, now numbered 800-802, were assigned to freight service on the Fargo Division. The 803 was assigned to the St. Paul Division. Alco's RS-1 model of the early 1940's was the nation's first road switcher type of locomotive adopted as the standard many years later. *Robert Anderson*

Three Alco RS-3s, 850-852, were purchased by the Northern Pacific in March 1953, followed by another four in December 1953, 853-856. By January 1955 four, 850-852 and 855, were assigned to the Fargo Division where they were operated in freight service. From time-to-time they substituted for 4-6-2 steamers, #2160, 2182, 2192 and 2223, in mixed train service out of Fargo. However, the 1600-horsepower RS-3s were not equipped with steam boilers, and they didn't need to be so equipped for this service, as the mixed train passenger cars were heated by stoves. *Robert Anderson*

Northern Pacific Locomotive Assignment
Yellowstone Division
- January 1955 -

Locomotive No.	Class / Type	Service	Notes
401, 408	DE Baldwin VO-1000	Leased	Foley Bros. Colstrip Mine
704	DE Alco S-2	Switcher	Laurel
705, 706	DE Alco S-2	Switcher	Mandan
707	DE Alco S-2	Switcher	Laurel
720-724	DE Alco S-4	Switcher	Billings
853-854	DE Alco RS-3	Freight	
1031	L-7 0-6-0	Switcher	Glendive
1186	G-2 0-8-0	Switcher	Laurel
1187	G-2 0-8-0	Switcher	Livingston Shop
1191-1193	G-2 0-8-0	Switcher	Laurel
1530, 1544, 1568, 1579	W 2-8-2	Switcher	Laurel
1580	W 2-8-2	Switcher	Forsyth
1627	W 2-8-2	Switcher	Laurel
1661	W-1 2-8-2	Freight	
1665	W-1 2-8-2	Freight	Shop - Glendive Roundhouse
1696	W-1 2-8-2	Freight	
1709	W-3 2-8-2	Freight	
1710	W-3 2-8-2	Freight	Stored awaiting disposition
1711	W-3 2-8-2	Freight	Transfer
1712, 1717-1718	W-3 2-8-2	Freight	
1720	W-3 2-8-2	Work	
1736, 1739, 1741, 1769, 1773	W-3 2-8-2	Freight	
1778	W-3 2-8-2	Freight	Stored - Mandan
1789, 1834	W-3 2-8-2	Freight	
1908, 1914, 1915	W-2 2-8-2	Freight	
1919	W-2 2-8-2	Work	
2228, 2232, 2238	Q-5 4-6-2	Passenger	
2254	Q-6 4-6-2	Passenger	
2500	W-4 2-8-2	Switcher	Mandan
2501-2505	W-4 2-8-2	Switcher	Glendive
2650-2651, 2656-2658	A-2 4-8-4	Freight	
2661, 2664, 2667	A-3 4-8-4	Freight	
2670-2672, 2675	A-4 4-8-4	Freight	
5007	Z-5 2-8-8-4	Freight	Stored - Glendive
5102, 5104	Z-6 4-6-6-4	Freight	
5106	Z-6 4-6-6-4	Freight	Shop - Livingston
5107-5109	Z-6 4-6-6-4	Freight	
5136, 5141-5143, 5146-5147, 5149	Z-8 4-6-6-4	Freight	

Northern Pacific Locomotive Assignment
Yellowstone Division (Continued)
- January 1955 -

Locomotive No.		Class / Type	Service	Notes
6000A-B-C-D	DE	EMD F3A/F3B/F3B/F3A	Freight	
6001A-B-C-D	DE	EMD F3A/F3B/F3B/F3A	Freight	
6002A-B-C-D	DE	EMD F3A/F3B/F3B/F3A	Freight	
6003A-B-C-D	DE	EMD F3A/F3B/F3B/F3A	Freight	
6004A-B-C-D	DE	EMD F3A/F3B/F3B/F3A	Freight	
6005A-B-C-D	DE	EMD F5A/F3B/F3B/F5A	Freight	
6006A-B-C-D	DE	EMD F5A/F3B/F3B/F5A	Freight	
6007A-B-C-D	DE	EMD F7A/F7B/F7B/F7A	Freight	
6008A-B-C-D	DE	EMD F7A/F7B/F7B/F7A	Freight	
6009A-B-C-D	DE	EMD F7A/F7B/F7B/F7A	Freight	
6010A-B-C-D	DE	EMD F7A/F7B/F7B/F7A	Freight	
6011A-B-C-D	DE	EMD F7A/F7B/F7B/F7A	Freight	
6012A-B-C-D	DE	EMD F7A/F7B/F7B/F7A	Freight	
6013A-B-C-D	DE	EMD F7A/F7B/F7B/F7A	Freight	
6014A-B-C-D	DE	EMD F7A/F7B/F7B/F7A	Freight	
6015A-B-C-D	DE	EMD F7A/F7B/F7B/F7A	Freight	
6016A-B-C-D	DE	EMD F7A/F7B/F7B/F7A	Freight	
6050B	DE	EMD F7B	Freight	Extra B-unit

COMBINATION FREIGHT AND PASSENGER—Here is the newest model of General Motors' versatile freight and heavy-duty passenger locomotive. Operating as a single unit of 1500 h.p. or in combinations of 3000, 4500 or 6000 h.p., the new F7 hauls 25 to 30% more tonnage, controls heavier tonnage with dynamic brakes, utilizes a broader range of Diesel fuels and provides increased train-heating capacity for passenger service.

Northern Pacific Railway
- Yellowstone Division -

Mandan N.D. to Billings, MT. (Main Line) . . . . 431.69 mi.
Billings to Livingston, MT. (Main Line) . . . . 114.15 mi.
Beach, N.D. to Ollie, MT. (Ollie Branch) . . . . 25.89 mi.
Glendive to Sidney, MT. (Sidney Branch) . . . . 54.40 mi.
Glendive to Brockway, MT. (Redwater Branch) . . . . 62.02 mi.
Nichols to Colstrip, MT. (Rosebud Branch) . . . . 30.35 mi.
Billings to Shepherd, MT. (Billings & Central Montana Branch) . . . . 12.60 mi.
Hesper to Rapelje, MT. (Lake Basin Branch) . . . . 38.19 mi.
Laurel to Red Lodge, MT. (Rocky Fork Branch) . . . . 44.24 mi.
Silesia to Bridger, MT. (Clarks Fork Branch) . . . . 19.62 mi.
Mission to Wilsall, MT. (Shields River Branch) . . . . 22.90 mi.
Trackage rights (Branch Line) . . . . 5.37 mi.

Yellowstone Division - Total Mileage . . . .   545.84 Main Lines - 315.58 Branch Lines

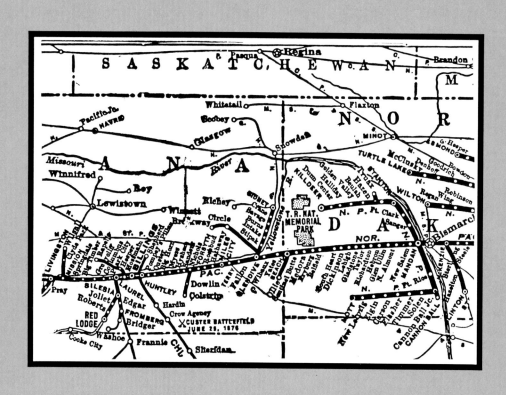

Assigned to switching service at the eastern end of the Yellowstone Division at Mandan, North Dakota, were a pair of Alco 1000-horsepower S-2 diesel switchers #705 and 706. The 705, with its winter cab extension in place, is shoving a home-road 40-foot double door box car into one of Mandan's yard tracks. *Dave Ingles photo - Al Chione collection*

Billings, Montana, at an elevation of 3,139-feet, has a large petro-chemical and oil refining industrial area. Alco S-4 #722, one of five assigned here, is switching a cut of large white tank cars filled with liquified petroleum gas. *Ed Fulcomer collection*

Prior to the pooling of cabooses each conductor had his own car. The cabooses were changed out at each crew change point, which was somewhat time consuming. It was each conductor's responsibility to keep his own caboose supplied, i.e. wrenches, fusees, chain, lanterns, etc. Class W-3 2-8-2 #1717 is working the caboose track filled with wooden cars at Forsyth, Montana in September 1956, while several of the crew members stand by. *Ed Gerlits*

During the mid-1950s, each box car or refer was still equipped with roof walks providing a means of reaching the brake wheels located at the top of one end of each car. Switching could be a very dangerous occupation for the brakeman if one wasn't always alert. "Mike" #1717 is switching a Pennsy box car at Forsyth, with one brakeman on the roof and another hanging on a grab iron while holding his footing in a stirrup. *Ed Gerlits*

A pair of Yellowstone Division assigned Baldwin VO-1000 switchers, 401 and 408, were leased to the Foley Brothers coal mining operation, which was owned by the Northwestern Improvement Co., a wholly owned subsidiary of the Northern Pacific Railway. This mining operation was conducted at the end of the Rosebud Branch which extended south from the main line near Forsyth to Colstrip, Montana, where large deposits of low-grade lignite coal was mined for use by the NP for their steam locomotives. *William J. Neill*

In 1955, the Laurel, Montana yards were assigned four Class G-2 USRA-type 0-8-0s, 1186 and 1191-1193, for heavy switching. There was much traffic interchanged at Laurel with the Chicago, Burlington & Quincy Railroad, their westernmost terminal. The 1186 and 1193 were both working the Laurel yard in September 1956. *Above: Ed Gerlits - Below: Al Chione collection*

Class W 2-8-2 #1530 was photographed working the Laurel yard in September 1956. Diesels had already bumped the "Mike" from freight to heavy switching service by the mid-1950s. *Ed Gerlits*

The American Locomotive Co. built 160 Class W 2-8-2 Mikados for the Northern Pacific between 1904 and 1907. One of these, #1544 assigned to the Yellowstone Division as a switch engine, is working at Mandan, N. D. in September 1955. Later in the day the heavy switcher will cross the Missouri River with a cut of cars and work industrial spurs in the Bismarck area, North Dakota's state capital. *Robert Bruneau*

During the mid-1950's, steam and diesel switchers worked side-by-side at most locations such as Laurel, Montana. Today the ex-NP Laurel yard is the major rail yard for the Montana Rail Link, a regional railroad established when many miles of the old NP was sold off by the Burlington Northern. Back in 1955, NP's Alco S-2 switchers represented the new generation switcher at Laurel. *Left: Ed Fulcomer coll. Below: R.R. Wallin collection*

In January 1955, Mikado #1720 was assigned to work train service, however by September 1956, the Class W-3 2-8-2 had returned to more familiar haunts, working freight in the Laurel, Montana vicinity. *Ed Gerlits*

A pair of December 1953-built Alco RS-3s, 853 and 854, were initially assigned as freight units on the Yellowstone Division. They were equipped for multiple-unit (MU) operation and were usually operated in pairs. RS-3 #853 shows off the graceful curves of Alco's 1600-horsepower road-switchers. *Tom Smart*

Class Q-6 4-6-2 #2254 was photographed on its way to the depot on September 9, 1955, after laying over between runs to-and-from St. Paul on coach passenger trains #3 (daily except Saturday) and 4 (daily except Sunday). The high stepping Pacific arrived at Mandan, North Dakota at 11:55 AM and is about to head back to St. Paul at 4:40 PM. *Robert Bruneau*

The Yellowstone Division was assigned a dozen 4-8-4s in January 1955, all in freight service. One of five Class A-2 Northerns, #2650, sits on the ready track at Forsyth, Montana with a full bunker of Rosebud coal which is mined in the area at Colstrip. The big, well maintained, Northern is just months from retirement. *Robert Brain*

The huge Class Z-8 4-6-6-4, #5149, spent nearly all of its fifteen-year career assigned on the Yellowstone Division where it worked the Glendive to Livingston segment easily handling 4,000-ton trains. The big Challenger type is slowly moving out to pick up its eastbound tonnage at Livingston on September 13, 1954. *Warren McGee*

Northern Pacific's twenty-one Z-6 class 4-6-6-4s were intended to replace lighter freight Mikado type 2-8-2 locomotives in the mountainous areas between Livingston, Montana and Spokane, Washington. One of these big roller-bearing equipped Challenger type locomotives, #5107, is working tonnage through the "Big Sky Country" near Livingston on March 15, 1956. *Warren McGee*

Challenger type #5107 is taking a well deserved break at Livingston in September 1956, before being refueled for another run. The big Z-6 4-6-6-4s were provided with Class 2-F semi-Vanderbilt tenders which carried 22,000-gallons of water and 27-tons of Montana's Rosebud coal. *Ed Gerlits*

Northern Pacific ordered eight Class A-3 4-8-4s from the Baldwin Locomotive Works, 2660-2667, in 1938, to replace the Class Q Pacifics which, in turn, replaced older 4-6-0s and 4-4-0s, which were retired. The A-3s were purchased as dual-purpose locomotives designed to pull either passenger or fast freight. With the introduction of diesel road power they were assigned more and more to freight service. A-3 #2664 is working a freight extra near Billings, Montana in September 1956.

The eight Baldwin-built Class A-4 locomotives, 2670-2677, were delivered just prior to WWII. These 4-8-4s, with their solid pilots, fold-up front couplers, all-weather cabs and massive 25,000-gallon tenders were awesome machines and were larger than NP's previous Northerns. Prior to being bumped by the new diesel road locomotives, they worked extensively in passenger service between St. Paul and Livingston. Now assigned primarily to freight, the 2675 was working tonnage at Laurel, Montana, while the 2672 (facing page), with its bell ringing caution for the many grade crossings, moves an extra freight through Billings, both in September 1956. *Three photos: Ed Gerlits*

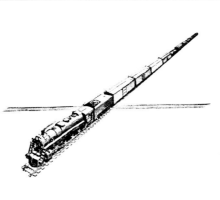

During the modern steam era, and eventually the diesel era, Livingston, Montana was one of the most important locations on the Northern Pacific. Located here was the heavy steam locomotive shops and later the major facility for the repair of the transcontinental diesel locomotive fleet. Above, Z-6 Class 4-6-6-4 Challenger, #5104, is pulling off of the long turntable and into the Livingston roundhouse for servicing on March 18, 1956. *Warren McGee*

Class Z-6 #5106, built by the American Locomotive Co. in October 1936, faces a relatively new EMD F9 freight diesel locomotive set at the Livingston roundhouse in September 1956. By this date all of the freight F9s had been delivered to the NP, but the big Challenger still had three years of service before being dismantled in October 1959. To many this was one of the most interesting times in railroading featuring the last of steam and first generation diesels. *Ed Gerlits*

On August 20, 1955, one of the big Z-8 Class 4-6-6-4s, #5147, is making about 40-mph with a unit coal drag near Tusler, Montana in the Yellowstone Valley just east of Miles City. This 5,250-ton freight extra has fifty Hart bottom-release gondolas which gross 105-tons each, the heavyweights of those days. *Warren McGee*

Northern Pacific EMD F-3, F-5 & F-7 Freight Locomotives
- January 1955 -

Previous Road No.	- 1950 - Renumbering	Model	Date Built	EMD Const. No.	Notes & Disposition
1st 6011A	2nd 6000A	F3-A	1/47	3779	Traded in to EMD for SD45, 6/67.
1st 6011B	2nd 6000B	F3-B	1/47	3874	To BN 701; Convt'd to Remote Receiver Car BN RCC 109, 5/72.
1st 6011C	2nd 6000C	F3-B	1/47	3875	To BN 763; Convt'd to Remote Receiver Unit RCU 5, 8/71, re# RCC 105.
1st 6011D	2nd 6000D	F3-A	1/47	3780	To BN 702; sold DES 3/81.
1st 6012A	2nd 6001A	F3-A	1/47	3781	To BN (704); Traded in to EMD for SD45, 4/70 by BN.
1st 6012B	2nd 6001B	F3-B	1/47	3876	Traded in to GE for U28C, 7/66.
1st 6012C	2nd 6001C	F3-B	1/47	3877	To BN 703; sold Precision National Corp., 9/74.
1st 6012D	2nd 6001D	F3-A	1/47	3782	Traded in to GE for U25C, 5/64.
1st 6013A	2nd 6002A	F3-A	1/47	3783	Traded in to GE for U25C, 7/64.
1st 6013B	2nd 6002B	F3-B	1/47	3878	To BN (705); Traded in to EMD for SD45, 6/70 by BN.
1st 6013C	2nd 6002C	F3-B	1/47	3879	To BN 707; sold to Precision National Corp., 11/71.
1st 6013D	2nd 6002D	F3-A	1/47	3784	Traded in to EMD for SD45, 7/66.
1st 6014A	2nd 6003A	F3-A	1/47	3785	Traded in to GE for U33C, 7/69.
1st 6014B	2nd 6003B	F3-B	1/47	3880	Traded in to EMD for SD45, 6/70 by BN.
1st 6014C	2nd 6003C	F3-B	1/47	3881	To BN 709; sold to Precision National Corp., 11/72.
1st 6014D	2nd 6003D	F3-A	1/47	3786	Traded in to EMD for SD45, 6/70 by BN.
1st 6015A	2nd 6004A	F3-A	1/47	4312	Traded in to GE for U25C, 7/64.
1st 6015B	2nd 6004B	F3-B	1/47	3882	Traded in to EMD for SD45, 6/70 by BN.
1st 6015C	2nd 6004C	F3-B	1/47	3883	Traded in to GE for U25C, 9/65.
1st 6015D	2nd 6004D	F3-A	1/47	4313	Traded in to EMD for SD45, 6/67.
1st 6016A	2nd 6005A	F5-A	10/48	6656	To BN 706; sold to Universal Machinery Co., 8/71.
1st 6504B to 1st 6016B	2nd 6005B	F3-B	1/47	3795	Converted to passenger unit 6553B 6/62 [See page 37]
1st 6503B to 1st 6016C	2nd 6005C	F3-B	1/47	3793	Re# 6025C [occasionally/temporarily]; To BN 711; sold to PNC., 11/71.
1st 6016D	2nd 6005D	F5-A	10/48	6657	Re# 6025D [occasionally/temporarily]; Traded in to GE for U25C, 9/65.
1st 6017A	2nd 6006A	F5-A	10/48	6658	Re# 6051A spare freight cab-unit, 10/59 [See 6051A on facing page]
1st 6505B to 1st 6017B	2nd 6006B	F3-B	1/47	3872	Converted to passenger 6551B, 12/59 [See page 37]
1st 6506B to 1st 6017C	2nd 6006C	F3-B	4/47	4788	Converted to passenger 6552B, 3/60 [See page 37]
1st 6017D	2nd 6006D	F5-A	10/48	6659	Re# 6052A spare freight cab-unit, 10/59 [See 6052A on facing page]
	2nd 6007A	F7-A	2/50	10908	To BN 710; sold to Naporano Bros. Iron & Metal Co., 12/72.
	2nd 6007B	F7-B	2/50	10920	Traded in to GE for U28C, 6/66.
	2nd 6007C	F7-B	2/50	10921	Converted to Remote Receiver Unit NP RCU 2, 6/68; To BN RCU 2, re# 1st BN RCU 102; wrecked - sold for scrap to Hyman Michaels, 8/72.
	2nd 6007D	F7-A	2/50	10909	To BN 712; Sold to Precision National Corp., 10/72.
	2nd 6008A	F7-A	2/50	10910	Traded in to GE for U25C, 9/65.
	2nd 6008B	F7-B	2/50	10922	To BN 713; Converted to Remote Receiver Unit BN RCU 111, 7/72; renumbered BN RCC 111, '73; sold to the British Columbia Ry., 3/80.
	2nd 6008C	F7-B	2/50	10923	To BN (715); Traded to EMD for SD45, 4/70 by BN.
	2nd 6008D	F7-A	2/50	10911	To BN 714; sold to Joseph Simon & Sons, 3/73.
	2nd 6009A	F7-A	2/50	10912	To BN 716; sold to Universal Machinery Co., 8/71.
	2nd 6009B	F7-B	2/50	10924	To BN 717; sold to Chrome Crankshaft, '81.
	2nd 6009C	F7-B	2/50	10925	To BN (719); Traded to EMD for SD45, 7/70 by BN.
	2nd 6009D	F7-A	2/50	10913	To BN 718; sold to Precision National Corp., 11/71.
	2nd 6010A	F7-A	2/50	10914	To BN 720; sold to Rail Car Corp./Colorado & Eastern Ry., '81, resold to Great Northern Transportation Corp., Denver, 2/87, sold for scrap '91..
	2nd 6010B	F7-B	2/50	10926	To BN 721; sold to Precision National Corp., 11/71.
	2nd 6010C	F7-B	2/50	10927	Converted to Remote Receiver Unit NP RCU 1, 12/68; To BN RCU 1; redesignated Remote Receiver Car and renumbered BN RCC 101, '73.
	2nd 6010D	F7-A	2/50	10915	Traded in to EMD for SD45, 3/67.

Road Numbers	Model	Date Built	EMD Const. No.	Notes & Disposition
2nd 6011A	F7-A	2/50	10916	To BN 722; sold to Universal Machinery Co., 8/71.
2nd 6011B	F7-B	2/50	10928	To BN (723); sold to Precision National Corp., 11/70.
2nd 6011C	F7-B	2/50	10929	To BN 725; sold to Rail Car Corp/Colorado & Eastern Ry., '81; scrap '91.
2nd 6011D	F7-A	2/50	10917	Traded to EMD for SD45, 7/70 by BN.
2nd 6012A	F7-A	2/50	10918	To BN 724; sold to Naporano Bros. Iron & Metal Co., 11/73.
2nd 6012B	F7-B	2/50	10930	To BN 727; sold to Precision National Corp., 10/71.
2nd 6012C	F7-B	2/50	10931	To BN 761; sold to Hyman-Michaels, '81.
2nd 6012D	F7-A	2/50	10919	Traded in to GE for U33C, 7/69.
2nd 6013A	F7-A	5/51	14252	Traded in to EMD for SD45, 6/70 by BN.
2nd 6013B	F7-B	5/51	14264	To BN 729; sold to Precision National Corp., 4/73.
2nd 6013C	F7-B	5/51	14265	To BN (731); Sold to Precision Engineering Co., 11/70; resold to the Chicago & Northwestern Ry. as electric slug C&NW BU-34, 2/71.
2nd 6013D	F7-A	5/51	14253	To BN 730; destroyed in South Seattle, Washington wreck, 10/77.
2nd 6014A	F7-A	5/51	14254	To BN 732; sold to Rail Car Corp./Colorado & Eastern Ry., '81; resold to Great Northern Trans. Co., Denver, 2/87; to Pielet Bros. McCook, Il. 1/91.
2nd 6014B	F7-B	5/51	14266	To BN 733; sold to Chrome Crankshaft, '81.
2nd 6014C	F7-B	5/51	14267	To BN 735; sold to General Metals, '81.
2nd 6014D	F7-A	5/51	14255	To BN 734; sold to Joseph Simon & Sons, 5/73.
2nd 6015A	F7-A	5/51	14256	To BN 736; Wrecked at Sheffels, Montana; sold to U. M. Co., 8/71.
2nd 6015B	F7-B	5/51	14268	To BN 737; sold to Chrome Crankshaft, 3/81.
2nd 6015C	F7-B	5/51	14269	To BN 739; sold to Naporano Bros. Iron & Metal Co., 12/72.
2nd 6015D	F7-A	5/51	14257	To BN 738; sold to Joseph Simon & Sons; '81.
2nd 6016A	F7-A	6/51	14258	To BN 740; sold to Naporano Bros. Iron & Metal Co., 6/74.
2nd 6016B	F7-B	6/51	14270	To BN 741; sold to Precision National Corp., 6/81.
2nd 6016C	F7-B	6/51	14271	To BN 743; sold to Joseph Simon & Sons; 3/73.
2nd 6016D	F7-A	6/51	14259	Traded in to GE for U33C, 7/69.
2nd 6017A	F7-A	6/51	14260	To BN 744; sold to Naporano Bros. Iron & Metal Co., '81.
2nd 6017B	F7-B	6/51	14272	To BN 745; sold to Precision National Corp., 11/71.
2nd 6017C	F7-B	6/51	14273	To BN (747); sold to Precision Engineering Co., 11/70.
2nd 6017D	F7-A	6/51	14261	To BN 746; sold to Naporano Bros. Iron & Metal Co., 11/73.
6018A	F7-A	6/51	14262	To BN 748; sold to Precision National Corp., 2/74.
6018B	F7-B	6/51	14274	To BN 749; Converted to Remote Receiver Unit BN RCU 107, 2/72; redesignated Remote Receiver Car, renumbered 2nd BN RCC 102, '72.
6018C	F7-B	6/51	14275	To BN 751; sold to Hyman-Michaels, '81.
6018D	F7-A	6/51	14263	To BN 750; sold to Joseph Simon & Sons, 3/73.
6019A	F7-A	12/51	15672	To BN 752; sold to Rail Car Corp./Colorado & Eastern Ry., '81; resold to GN Trans., 2/87; to Locomotive Maintenance Inc., Minneapolis, 3/88.
6019B	F7-B	12/51	15676	To BN 753; sold to Rail Car Corp./Colorado & Eastern Ry., '81; resold to GN Trans., 2/87, to Locomotive Maintenance Inc., Minneapolis, 1/91.
6019C	F7-B	12/51	15677	To BN 755; sold to Precision Engineering Co., 11/70; resold to the Chicago & Northwestern Ry. as electric slug C&NW BU-32, 2/71.
6019D	F7-A	12/51	15673	To BN 754; sold to Precision National Corp., 4/73.
6020A	F7-A	12/51	15674	To BN 756; sold to Precision Engineering Co., 1/71.
6020B	F7-B	12/51	15678	To BN 757; sold to Precision National Corp., 4/73.
6020C	F7-B	12/51	15679	To BN 759; sold to Joseph Simon & Sons, 3/73.
6020D	F7-A	12/51	15675	To BN 758; sold to Joseph Simon & Sons, 7/80.
6050B	F7-B	12/51	15680	[Purchased as a spare B-unit.] Traded in to GE for U33C, 7/69.
[6051A]	F5-A	10/48	6658	[From 2nd 6006A, 10/59] To BN 760; sold to Nap. Bros. I. & M. Co., 6/74.
[6052A]	F5-A	10/48	6659	[From 2nd 6006D, 10/59] To BN 762; sold to Universal Machine Co., 8/71.

Northern Pacific F3 #6000A is on lease to the Colorado & Southern Railway and was photographed at C&S's Rice Yard at Denver in November 1960. A few of NP's F3s also made it to Colorado, Kansas, Texas etc., through lease to the Rock Island during the 1960s. *Ken Crist*

With the relative success experienced with their first eleven FT diesel road locomotives, the management of the Northern Pacific decided to purchase more road locomotives, both passenger and freight. By this time, late 1946, the Electro-Motive Division of General Motors Corp. had produced a 1500-horsepower road diesel unit, the F3. This new F3 was available as two, three or four unit locomotives, offering several gear ratios for the speed of passenger service or the power for freight operation. After testing EMD's 3-unit F3 demonstrator #754 in main line service during late 1946, the NP ordered five 4-unit locomotives for freight service. They were initially assigned to the Yellowstone Division, where they bumped many of the 5000 series, Class Z-5 2-8-8-4 steam locomotives to helper service on the Rocky Mountain Division. NP's first pair of F3 cab-units, 2nd #6000A and #6000D, are presented on this page. The 6000D is at Laurel with an F3B and F7B. *Ed Fulcomer collection*

The first five F3 locomotives were originally numbered after the eleven FT locomotives as NP 6011 through 6015. In December 1949 and January 1950, most road locomotives were renumbered into slots indicated by their respective horsepower ratings. The 5400-hp four-unit FT locomotives were renumbered in the 5400 series, while the four-unit freight F-3 locomotives became 2nd 6000 through 6004. Thus, the 6000A+C, photographed at Livingston were originally 6011A+C. *Bruce Butler photo - Jerry Quinn collection*

Northern Pacific's original freight F3s were typical Phase I models, with four high cooling fans and three portholes on both the cab and booster units. They were equipped with dynamic brakes, but without the single front dynamic brake fan. The railroad added nose lift rings and a winterization hatch covering the rear fan. Of the ten freight Phase I F3 cab units having three portholes, such as the 6003A, only two A-units, 6000D and 6001A, made it to the Burlington Northern merger of March 1970. *R.R. Wallin collection*

NP 2nd 6003C, originally 6014C prior to January 1950, illustrates a typical Phase I F3 booster unit with a back-up light on the rear of the unit and a host of multiple-unit connections. The freight B-units advertised that this was the *Main Street of the Northwest*. These ten freight B-units, 6011B+C through 6015B+C, later 6000B+C through 6004B+C, were delivered without steam generators but with the necessary piping in case boilers were ever added for passenger service. This never happened. The 6003C was at Minneapolis in May 1970, just after the BN merger, and was about to be renumbered as BN 709.
Dave Ingles photo - Al Chione collection

In early 1948, two additional four-unit F3 freight locomotives were ordered. However, during this period the NP realized the inconvenience of turning the A-B-B passenger locomotive sets at St. Paul and Seattle after each run. It was decided to make some exchanges among present and brand new units then on order. Passenger F-3 booster-units, 6503B through 6506B, were converted to freight service and renumbered 1st 6016B+C and 6017B+C. The order was changed to eight new F3 (NP designation F5) cab-units, four passenger, 2nd 6503C - 6506C, to take the place of 1st 6503C - 6506C which became 2nd 6503B - 6506B, and four freight cab-units, 1st 6016A+D and 6017A+D. These were delivered in October 1948. To further complicate matters even more, the F5A/F3B/F3B/F5A locomotives, 1st 6016 and 6017, were renumbered 2nd 6005 and 6006 fifteen months later. NP F5A/F3B, 2nd 6005, were at Duluth to help with iron ore movements on July 6, 1954, the same month the NP began to add Alphabet letters A through D to their locomotives. The other two units of the locomotive set of 6005, operating separately, were temporarily renumbered 6025 to prevent confusion. With the addition of the Alpha letters A + D to the cab units this renumbering was deemed unnecessary. Notice also that the 6005 has the original "Northern Pacific" surrounding the Monad. This was changed to "Northern Pacific Railway" also in 1954. *Dr. A.G. Chione*

NP 2nd 6000A, originally 1st 6011A, the road's first freight F3A, along with 2nd 6005C, converted from passenger 1st 6503B, was at Livingston. Notice the freight B-unit's ex-passenger steam boiler roof vents and piping. *Matthew J. Herson*

NORTHERN PACIFIC RAILWAY
Main Street of the Northwest

Northern Pacific F5A #6005A, the same unit as pictured at the top of page 70 (facing page), is again working the eastern end of the system in August 1962. Notice the Alphabet "A" added to the number board and modern "Northern Pacific Railway" applied around the Monad. Nose lift rings are also a later addition. The 6005A and an F7B are on an eastbound freight as it hits the Soo Line diamonds at Detroit Lakes, Minnesota. *Russ Porter*

In October 1959, the F5A/F3B/F3B/F5A freight set, 2nd 6006, were broken up to provide two spare freight F5A cab units and two extra F3B passenger booster units. The F5 cab units were renumbered 6051A and 6052A. This renumbering did not take place until 1959, but included here for completeness. There were no 6051B-C-D or 6052B-C-D. The 6051A was photographed at St. Paul, while the 6052A was at Minneapolis. There is some modelers information here. Recognizing that all units are not exactly the same, notice that the 6051A has yellow nose lift rings and no "Radio Equipped" logo, while the 6052A has black lift rings and "Radio Equipped" lettering and lightning bolt stencils. *Two photos: Dave Ingles - Al Chione collection*

From time-to-time one of the four-unit locomotives from one of the western division's would be temporarily transferred east to help with transporting iron ore. Prior to the Alpha letters being added to the cab units, one half of the locomotive set, one of the cab and booster units, usually the "D" and "C" units, would be renumbered 6025D and 6025C. After the Alpha letters were added in 1954/55, an A-B-B-A locomotive was simply broken up making two A-B sets, such as the two F7 3,000-hp locomotives, 6015A-B and 6015D-C, at Duluth's engine terminal. *Russ Porter*

On a gray, overcast afternoon in May 1960, a perfect F7 A-B-B-A set, 2nd 6011A-B-C-D, moves to pick up tonnage at Portland for a northbound run to Auburn, Washington. The F-units began to be mixed after the Alpha letters were added during 1954 and 1955. *R.R. Wallin collection*

The engineer of an eastbound manifest inspects his train on a slight curve as it is about to cross the single track Soo Line at Detroit Lakes, Minnesota in August 1962. His four-unit locomotive consists of F7A #6013A, an F3-A, F3-B and another F7A.
Russ Porter photo - Ed Fulcomer collection

Above: Northern Pacific's Train #603, a St. Paul to Auburn manifest, works through Big Timber, Montana, between Laurel and Livingston, as Extra-6002-West on February 19, 1956. This train picks up CB&Q traffic at Laurel and makes set outs at Missoula, Spokane and Pasco where it makes a Portland connection with SP&S Train #275. *Warren McGee*

Right: A trio of pristine EMD Phase I F3s have taken advantage of the free parking afforded by the City of Fargo, North Dakota in August 1962. An engine maintainer is climbing the grab irons on the engineer's side in order to clean the cab-unit's windshields. *Russ Porter*

- Northern Pacific Freight F-Units -
A Pictorial Perspective

Northern Pacific's first road diesel freight locomotives consisted of eleven 4-unit FT sets originally numbered 6000-6010. They were renumbered in December 1949 and January 1950, to 5400-5410 representing the locomotive horsepower. The FT's were identified by their four portholes and flat rectangular dynamic brake grid housings atop each unit. Large number boards and oscillating headlights were added by the railroad's shop forces. The 5401A was at Middle Yard, Seattle on September 4, 1961. *Dave Ingles photo - Joe Shine collection*

The second type of road freight locomotive purchased by the NP was five sets of EMD Phase I F3s, 6011-6015. When the FTs were renumbered from the 6000 series to the 5400 series, the original freight F3s were renumbered as 2nd 6000-6004. These Phase I F3s were identified by their high fans, wire screens and three portholes on both the cab and booster units. F3A+B 6003A and 6002B along with F7A 6010A are at Livingston. *Matthew J. Herson*

Four later model freight F3As, designated as an F5A on the NP, were acquired in October 1948, as cab units for two additional freight locomotives, 1st 6016A+D and 1st 6017A+D. The four booster units for these two sets, 6016B+C and 6017B+C, were converted from passenger F3B units. They were renumbered as 2nd 6005 and 2nd 6006. These F5As had lower fans which were interchangeable with earlier F3s, as seen on the 6005A. The F5s, with their stainless steel grills and two portholes on the cab units, looked more like an F7 than an F3. The 6005A is at Minneapolis. *Ed Kanak photo - Ed Fulcomer collection*

The fourteen freight F7 locomotives, 6007-6020, and spare F7B #6050B, were all delivered between February 1950 and December 1951. Like the F5s, they had lower roof fans, stainless steel grills and the cab units had only two portholes. EMD F7A 6015A was photographed at Laurel, Montana. *K.C. Henkels photo - Ed Fulcomer collection*

Following the F7s, the Northern Pacific purchased fifteen freight F9 four-unit locomotives, 7000-7014. They were all acquired between January 1954 and March 1956. Other than the road number, the only identifying feature on the F9s were an additional air-filter vent just ahead of the first porthole. F9A #7003D was photographed at Laurel. *K.C. Henkels*

Northern Pacific Locomotive Assignment
Rocky Mountain Division
- January 1955 -

Locomotive No.	Class	/ Type	Service	Notes
23	Y-1	2-8-0	Switcher	Helena
25	Y-1	2-8-0	Switcher	Stored - Butte
28	Y-1	2-8-0	Switcher	Stored awaiting disposition
31	Y	2-8-0	Switcher	Helena
33, 36	Y	2-8-0	Switcher	Missoula
42	Y	2-8-0	Switcher	Helena
564-568	DE	EMD GP7	Freight	
569	DE	EMD GP7	Passenger	
708-709, 711-712	DE	Alco S-2	Switcher	Missoula
718-719	DE	Alco S-4	Switcher	Butte
1057	L-9	0-6-0	Switcher	Stored - Livingston
1093	L-9	0-6-0	Switcher	Bozeman
1188	G-2	0-8-0	Switcher	Livingston
1189	G-2	0-8-0	Switcher	Shop - Livingston Roundhouse
1351	S-4	4-6-0	Freight	
1356, 1379	S-4	4-6-0	Freight	Stored awaiting disposition
1382	S-4	4-6-0	Freight	
1387	S-4	4-6-0	Freight	Stored awaiting disposition
1522	W	2-8-2	Freight	Shop - Missoula Roundhouse
1536, 1562	W	2-8-2	Freight	
1591	W	2-8-2	Switcher	Livingston
1624	W	2-8-2	Freight	Stored awaiting disposition
1634	W	2-8-2	Switcher	Livingston
1638	W	2-8-2	Freight	Stored awaiting disposition
1719	W-3	2-8-2	Freight	
1733	W-3	2-8-2	Freight	Helper
1761	W-3	2-8-2	Freight	
1767, 1808	W-3	2-8-2	Freight	Stored awaiting disposition
1809	W-3	2-8-2	Freight	Shop - Missoula Roundhouse
1811	W-3	2-8-2	Freight	Stored awaiting disposition
1814-1815	W-3	2-8-2	Freight	
1818	W-3	2-8-2	Freight	Helper
1838	W-5	2-8-2	Freight	Stored - Helena
1840	W-5	2-8-2	Freight	Stored - Missoula
1842	W-5	2-8-2	Freight	Stored - Helena
1843	W-5	2-8-2	Freight	Stored awaiting disposition
1855-1856	W-5	2-8-2	Freight	Helper
1858	W-5	2-8-2	Freight	Shop - Helena Roundhouse
2163	Q-3	4-6-2	Passenger	
2212	Q-4	4-6-2	Passenger	
2245	Q-5	4-6-2	Passenger	Stored - Butte
2681, 2687	A-5	4-8-4	Passenger	

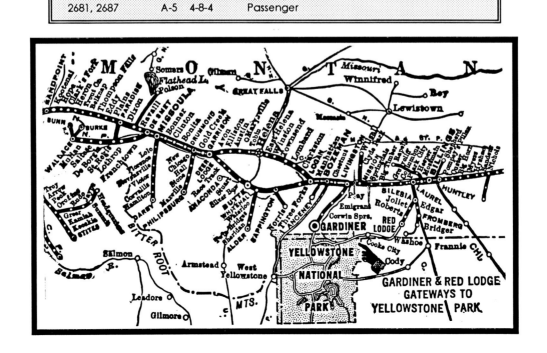

GARDINER & RED LODGE GATEWAYS TO YELLOWSTONE PARK

Northern Pacific Locomotive Assignment
Rocky Mountain Division (Continued)
- January 1955 -

Locomotive No.	Class / Type		Service	Notes
4020	Z-3	2-8-8-2	Freight	Stored - Wallace, ID.
4021	Z-3	2-8-8-2	Freight	Helper
4025	Z-3	2-8-8-2	Freight	Shop - Missoula Roundhouse
4501	Z-4	2-8-8-2	Freight	Stored - Helena
5001	Z-5	2-8-8-4	Freight	Stored - Livingston
5002	Z-5	2-8-8-4	Freight	Helper
5004	Z-5	2-8-8-4	Freight	Stored - Helena
5005-5006	Z-5	2-8-8-4	Freight	Stored - Livingston
5100	Z-6	4-6-6-4	Freight	Stored - Livingston
5101, 5103	Z-6	4-6-6-4	Freight	Stored - Missoula
5120	Z-6	4-6-6-4	Freight	
5121	Z-7	4-6-6-4	Freight	Stored - Livingston
5122-5123	Z-7	4-6-6-4	Freight	Stored awaiting disposition
5124	Z-7	4-6-6-4	Freight	Stored - Livingston
5125	Z-7	4-6-6-4	Freight	Stored awaiting disposition
5126	Z-7	4-6-6-4	Freight	Stored - Livingston
5133-5134	Z-8	4-6-6-4	Freight	
5401A-B-C-D	DE FTA/FTB/FTB/FTA		Freight	
5408A-B-C-D	DE FTA/FTB/FTB/FTA		Freight	
6017A-B-C-D	DE F7A/F7B/F7B/F7A		Freight	
7000A-B-C-D	DE F9A/F9B/F9B/F9A		Freight	
7001A-B-C-D	DE F9A/F9B/F9B/F9A		Freight	
7002A-B-C-D	DE F9A/F9B/F9B/F9A		Freight	
7003A-B-C-D	DE F9A/F9B/F9B/F9A		Freight	
7004A-B-C-D	DE F9A/F9B/F9B/F9A		Freight	
7005A-B-C-D	DE F9A/F9B/F9B/F9A		Freight	
7006A-B-C-D	DE F9A/F9B/F9B/F9A		Freight	

Northern Pacific Railway
- Rocky Mountain Division -

Livingston to Helena, MT. (Main Line) . . . . 124.29 mi.
Helena to Paradise, MT. via the St. Regis cutoff (Main Line) . . . . 219.00 mi.
Logan to Butte, MT. (Main Line) . . . . 69.98 mi.
Butte to Garrison, MT. (Main Line - Leased) . . . . 52.01 mi.
DeSmet to Paradise, MT. (Main Line) . . . . 64.02 mi.
Livingston to Gardiner, MT. (Park Branch) . . . . 54.26 mi.
Manhatten to Anceney, MT. (Camp Creek Branch) . . . . 15.20 mi.
Sappington to Norris, MT. (Red Bluff Branch) . . . . 21.33 mi.
Whitehall to Alder, MT. (Ruby Valley Branch) . . . . 45.60 mi.
Drummond to Philpsburg, MT. (Philpsburg Branch) . . . . 25.95 mi.
Missoula to Darby, MT. (Bitter Root Branch) . . . . 65.44 mi.
Dixon to Polson, MT. (Flathead Valley Branch) . . . . 32.94 mi.
St. Regis; Haugan, MT. to Wallace, ID. (Coeur d'Alene Branch) . . . . 39.82 mi.
St. Regis to Haugan, MT. (Branch Line - Milwaukee Road - Leased) . . . . 18.62 mi.
Wallace, ID. (Burke Branch) . . . . 0.31 mi.
Joint trackage in Burke, ID. . . . . 0.36 mi.
Wallace to Bunn, ID. (Sunset Branch) . . . . 3.27 mi.
Wallace to Burke, ID. (Branch Line - Union Pacific - Leased) . . . . 6.21 mi.

Rocky Mountain Division - Total Mileage . . . . 529.30 Main Lines - 329.31 Branch Lines

On our roster date, Class L-9 switcher #1057 was stored at Livingston, however just a few days earlier, on December 23, 1954, it was switching at Bozeman, Montana. In January 1955, It had been replaced at Bozeman by another L-9 0-6-0, #1093. *Warren McGee photo - Al Chione collection*

Class W-5 2-8-2 #1855, heavy with smoke box pumps, was assigned to helper service on the Rocky Mountain Division in January 1955, but by September 6th it was working with an auxiliary tank, in local freight service, through Staples, Minnesota. *Robert Bruneau*

It's a calm day in Livingston, the temperature is 20-degrees Fahrenheit and the 5126, a Class Z-7 4-6-6-4, has but 10 days left on her flue date, then she will be set aside and later sent to the scrap pile. On February 19, 1956, the big Challenger is earning her keep as she leaves town with 113 cars/6000 tons tied to her tender. Bozeman Pass is in the distance over her stack, a location she has crossed many times, but will never traverse again. Extra-5126-East is heading for Laurel, then she will be forwarded to Brainerd where she was scrapped on September 14, 1956.
Two photos: Warren McGee

Below: On June 24, 1956, another Z-7 waits for a call at Livingston. Unlike most other classes of Northern Pacific locomotives, the six Class Z-7 Challengers, built by Alco in late 1941, spent their entire careers on the Rocky Mountain Division. They worked primarily in heavy freight service but on occasion, especially during WWII, they would be called to operate heavy passenger and troop trains to avoid excessive double heading west of Livingston. *Al Chione collection*

All twenty-one Class Z-6 4-6-6-4 Challengers were assigned to the Rocky Mountain and Idaho Divisions where they worked west of Livingston. About one-half of the Z-6s worked the 240 route miles between Livingston and Missoula via Helena, where they routinely handled 4,000-ton trains without a helper. The other half operated 3,200-ton trains at 50-mph over one percent grades between Pasco and Parkwater (Spokane), Washington. Challenger #5120, the highest numbered Z-6, is about to leave Livingston with westbound tonnage in December 1948. *Warren McGee photo - Al Chione collection*

During January 1955, Class W-5 2-8-2 #1842 was stored at Helena, Montana during the normal January slack period. By August 1957, the Mikado was in local freight service, working out of Rice Point Yard at Duluth. Note the interesting Northern Pacific express car just behind the tender. *Russ Porter*

Extra-5101-West is about to cut off its helper engine "on-the-fly", note the rear brakeman on the caboose porch, at Muir, Montana, the East portal of Bozeman Tunnel. The Z-5 Class 2-8-8-4 Yellowstones, such as the 5004, were normally assigned as pushers between Livingston and Bozeman Tunnel. *Warren McGee*

Class W-3 2-8-2 #1733 was also assigned to helper service on the Rocky Mountain Division in early 1955. By this late date there were only four Mikados remaining in helper service on the division, W-3s #1733 and #1818 along with W-5s #1855 and 1856. The "Mike" has been watered and just received a full bunker of coal for its next assignment. *Fred Scott*

The roller-bearing equipped Class Z-7 Challengers were initially assigned to the Rocky Mountain Division where they augmented Z-6 4-6-6-4s 5100-5109. The 5126, a Z-7, works in 20-degree weather 3-miles east of Livingston on February 19, 1956. The Northern Pacific well maintained their modern steam power until the end during the late 1950s. *Warren McGee*

The twelve Class Z-5 2-8-8-4s were built for and assigned to the Yellowstone Division's First and Second subdivisions between Glendive and Mandan through the "Bad Lands", where 216 miles of undulating track with one-percent grades faced both eastbound and westbound traffic. With the coming of the modern diesel road locomotives most of the Yellowstones were transferred to the Rocky Mountain Division at Livingston where they usually worked in helper service to Bozeman Tunnel. Z-5 #5004 is resting between helper assignments at the Livingston engine terminal on September 13, 1954.
Warren McGee photo - Al Chione collection

Engineer Ebert has the huge Z-7 #5121 under control as the eastbound extra climbs out of Dehart, near Big Timber on November 24, 1955, under a beautiful Montana sky. During this period the big Challengers worked side-by-side in freight service with the modern diesel road locomotives. *Warren McGee*

Northern Pacific's twenty-one Class Z-6 early Challenger type 4-6-6-4s, with their smaller tenders, were assigned to the Yellowstone, Rocky Mountain and Idaho Divisions during the mid-1950s. A Rocky Mountain Division Z-6, #5101, is working the westbound grade out of Livingston during the summer of 1954. The sights and sounds of these big steamers working the mountain grades were fondly remembered by the folks along the NP main line for decades after their demise. This was railroading! *Warren McGee photo - Al Chione collection*

In January 1955, the Rocky Mountain Division had only six diesel switchers assigned. All were Alcos, four S-2s and two S-4s. Alco S-2 #708 along with 709, 711 and 712, were assigned to Missoula, Montana. *Robert C. Anderson*

Rocky Mountain Division Alco S-4s 718 and 719 were assigned to work as switchers at Butte. Missoula and Butte were the only two cities on the division to have diesel switchers assigned in early 1955. *Ed Fulcomer collection*

Page 86 Above: Extra-5126-East is at Mission Wye, about six miles east of Livingston on February 19, 1956. Engineer Harold Moddrell has the big Challenger, with 113-cars and 6,000-tons, up to speed and will soon ease off to avoid higher speeds and will then use the drifting throttle. The temperature is hovering around the 20-degree mark. *Warren McGee*

Page 86 Below: Westbound empties are passing through Mission, Montana on April 21, 1956. Within about ten minutes Challenger Z-7 #5124 will bring the manifest to a its western terminus at Livingston, the division point of the Rocky Mountain Division. *Warren McGee*

Dayton was at the end of a NP branch reaching into southeastern Washington. The town was served by both the Northern Pacific and Union Pacific. Above, NP GP7 #566 along with local caboose #1537, a unique car used to handle Railway Express business, are sitting in front of the Dayton depot. The UP local has arrived with a GP7, below, and the NP local, with GP7 #564 and caboose #1537, is returning to Walla Walla "Caboose Hop". Dayton featured street running, but today the Burlington Northern has pulled out of the Walla Walla country and the UP lines are leased to and operated by a Watco operation, the Blue Mountain Railroad. In January 1955, both NP GP7s were assigned to the Rocky Mountain Division, but were working further west on the Idaho Division. *Two Photos: Bruce Butler*

Northern Pacific purchased five GP7s, 564-568, delivered in December 1953, equipped with dynamic brakes and 1,600 gallon fuel tanks for freight service on the Rocky Mountain Division. Two of these GP7s, 566 and 567, are assigned to local freight service out of Butte on April 27, 1958. *Montague Powell*

NP 569, the last of twenty GP7s, was equipped with dynamic brakes and a steam boiler with a pair of 800 gallon tanks, one for fuel and the other for water. The steam equipment was subsequently removed and the 569 became just another local freight locomotive. In March 1965, a "flying switch" with a grain hopper turned out to be a less than successful move. "What do we do now, Ollie?" *Bruce Butler*

In January 1955, the Rocky Mountain Division was assigned two 4-unit FT locomotives, 5401 and 5408. One half of the 5401 set, 5401D+C, are teamed up with a pair of F7s and a GP7 on an eastbound freight through Plains, Montana. The NP did not replace the drawbar coupling between the FT cab and booster units as most roads did, so you would always see FTs in at least an A-B lash-up. *Left:* The same FT set rests at Auburn in July 1965. About the only carbody modifications the NP made on their FTs were the addition of large number boards at 45-degree angles and the addition of a second headlight. The square dynamic brake roof grid housings was a unique feature to the FT units.
Above: Bruce Butler
Left: Matthew J. Herson

Above: Following the Clark Fork River through Lolo National Forest in western Montana, Extra-7000A-East, a four-unit F9 locomotive set, works tonnage through Thompson Falls on a cold but clear Montana day. As of January 1955, there were only seven 4-unit freight F9 locomotives on the system and all were assigned to main line service on the Rocky Mountain Division. *Bruce Butler*

An F9A, #7002D and F7B #6018B, have just taken a spin on the turntable at Minneapolis and are slowly backing onto a ready track where additional units will be added to their consist. *Dave Ingles photo - Al Chione collection*

Train #603, Northern Pacific's hot Twin Cities to West Coast manifest, is passing through Connell on May 21, 1961. There is a clear order board and operator G.L. Allen gives the fast freight a "roll-by" in front of this eastern Washington depot. Before long the 7002A-West will be arriving at Pasco for a crew change, then it's on to Auburn. *Bruce Butler*

In January 1955, the Rocky Mountain Division had only one F7 locomotive set assigned, the 6017. One half of the set, 6017A+B, have made it as far east as Minneapolis, where they are being turned on the table in April 1955. Note the, now obsolete, original "Northern Pacific" around the Monad. *Al Chione collection*

Eastbound Northern Pacific train #602, operating as Extra-7006D-East, is passing through the picturesque setting at Jens, Montana in the Clark Fork River Valley on June 4, 1955. This train left Auburn at 2:30 AM, picks up and sets out at Pasco, Spokane, Missoula, Helena, Laurel, Dilworth, Staples and arrives in the Twin Cities at 8:00 PM on the fourth evening. *Warren McGee*

Northern Pacific Locomotive Assignment
Idaho Division
- January 1955 -

Locomotive No.	Class / Type		Service	Notes
200-203	DE	EMD GP9	Leased	Camas Prairie R.R.
402, 404, 407, 410-411, 415, 418, 420	DE	Baldwin VO-1000	Switcher	Yardley
500	DE	Baldwin DRS 4-4-15	Passenger	
525	DE	Baldwin DRS 6-6-15	Freight	
552-555	DE	EMD GP7	Freight	
556	DE	EMD GP7	Passenger	
560-563	DE	EMD GP7	Freight	
1092	L-9	0-6-0	Leased	Camas Prairie R.R.
1171	G-1	0-8-0	Switcher	Pasco
1174, 1176, 1180	G-2	0-8-0	Switcher	Pasco
1201	Y-3	2-8-0	Switcher	Pasco
1250	Y-2	2-8-0	Switcher	Pasco
1254	Y-2	2-8-0	Switcher	Yardley
1264	Y-2	2-8-0	Switcher	Pasco
1353	S-4	4-6-0	Freight	
1354	S-4	4-6-0	Switcher	Yakima
1355	S-4	4-6-0	Freight	Shop - Parkwater Roundhouse
1358	S-4	4-6-0	Freight	
1359	S-4	4-6-0	Freight	Stored awaiting disposition
1360	S-4	4-6-0	Freight	
1362	S-4	4-6-0	Freight	Stored awaiting disposition
1365-1366, 1374-1376	S-4	4-6-0	Freight	
1377	S-4	4-6-0	Freight	Stored awaiting disposition
1516	W	2-8-2	Freight	Stored awaiting disposition
1521, 1533	W	2-8-2	Freight	
1546	W	2-8-2	Switcher	Pasco
1575, 1592, 1616, 1639	W	2-8-2	Freight	
1667	W-1	2-8-2	Freight	
1697	W-1	2-8-2	Leased	Camas Prairie R.R.
1722, 1725, 1729, 1735, 1738, 1742, 1770, 1781, 1787-1788, 1792, 1795, 1810, 1816, 1831	W-3	2-8-2	Freight	
1902	W-2	2-8-2	Freight	
1904	W-2	2-8-2	Freight	Stored - Parkwater
1912	W-2	2-8-2	Freight	
2256	Q-6	4-6-2	Passenger	
2689	A-5	4-8-4	Passenger	
5111-5119	Z-6	4-6-6-4	Freight	
5130-5132, 5135, 5137-5140	Z-8	4-6-6-4	Freight	
5144-5145	Z-8	4-6-6-4	Freight	Stored awaiting disposition
5148	Z-8	4-6-6-4	Freight	

Northern Pacific Railway
- Idaho Division -

Paradise, MT. to Yakima, WA. (Main Line) . . . . 419.76 mi.
Gibbon to Parker, WA. (Alternate Mail Line) . . . . 45.88 mi.
Hauser to Coeur d'Alene, ID. (Fort Sherman Branch) . . . . 13.39 mi.
Marshall, WA. to Arrow, ID. (Palouse & Lewiston Branch) . . . . 123.77 mi.
Belmont to Farmington, WA. (Farmington Branch) . . . . 5.61 mi.
Pullman Junction, WA. to Genesse, ID. (Genesse Branch) . . . . 27.64 mi.
Cheney to Coulee City and Adrian, WA. (Washington Central Branch) . . . . 128.60 mi.
Davenport to Eleanor, WA. (Seattle Branch) . . . . 17.92 mi.
Connell to Adco, WA. (Connell Northern Branch) . . . . 61.21 mi.
Basset Junction to Schrag, MT. (Ritzville Branch) . . . . 12.54 mi.
Snake River Jct. to Riparia, MT. (Snake River Branch) . . . . 40.96 mi.
Pasco to Villard Jct. and Wallula to Wallula Jct., WA. (Wallula Branch) . . . . 6.04 mi.
Attalia to Dayton, WA. (Dayton Branch) . . . . 86.09 mi.
Eureka to Pleasant View, WA. (Eurika Branch) . . . . 19.73 mi.
Tracy Junction to Tracy, WA. (Tracy Branch) . . . . 3.79 mi.
Zangar Junction, WA. to Pendleton, OR. (Pendleton Branch) . . . . 35.66 mi.
Smeltz to Athena, OR. (Athena Branch) . . . . 14.54 mi.
Trackage in Kennewick, WA. (Branch Line) . . . . 0.28 mi.
Toppenish to White Swan, WA. (Simcoe Branch) . . . . 19.99 mi.
Trackage rights and joint trackage (Branch Lines) . . . . 52.89 mi.

Idaho Division - Mileage . . . . 465.64 Main Lines - 670.65 Branch Lines

CAMAS PRAIRIE RAILROAD - Northern Pacific/Union Pacific Owned

Riparia, WA. to Stites, ID. . . . . 150.36 mi.
Spalding to Grangeville, ID. . . . . 66.79 mi.
Orofino to Headquarters, ID. . . . . 40.64 mi.

Idaho Division - Total Branch Line Mileage . . . . 928.44 mi.

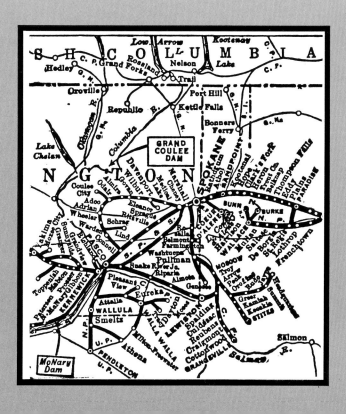

During January 1955, the yard at Yardley (Spokane) had nine switchers assigned, eight Baldwin diesels and this Class Y-2 #1254. It is almost unbelievable, but when new in 1901 and 1902, these minuscule Consolidation-type 2-8-0s handled main line freight on the Idaho and Rocky Mountain Divisions. There were several in each train in the mountainous territory.
Gayle Christen

While all of the diesel switchers assigned to Yardley in early 1955 were Baldwin VO-1000s, they did not all look exactly alike. The 420, was a "four-stacker", while the 410, below, with nearly the same body style, had but a single exhaust stack.
Left: Alan Miller - Below: Jerry Quinn

In 1955, the Idaho Division had a total of thirteen S-4 Class 4-6-0 locomotives, all assigned to the many local freights operating in Idaho and eastern Washington. During January, the 1355 was spending some shop time in the Parkwater roundhouse, but it was soon back at work in branch line service. The S-4s were strictly Western locomotives, as during most of their careers the forty Baldwin built Ten-Wheelers, in the 1350-1389 series, were never assigned east of the Rocky Mountain Division. *Dr. A.G. Chione*

The 2-8-2 was another wheel arrangement very prevalent on the Idaho Division during the mid-1950s. There were eight Class W, two Class W-1, three Class W-2 and fifteen Class W-3 locomotives available for freight and heavy switching service in January 1955. Mikado #1521, was one of six active Class W locomotives assigned to freight service on the Idaho Division. *Jerry Quinn collection*

In January 1955, Mikado #1725 was one of the Class W-3 2-8-2s assigned to the Idaho Division for freight service. By July 30, 1957, the "Mike" was still hard at work for the NP, but now at the eastern end of the system, on the Lake Superior Division, where it was photographed running light at Superior, Wisconsin. *Ed Spitzer*

Mikado #1795 was another Class W-3 2-8-2 which moved east from the Idaho Division. The locomotive is taking on water near the Rices Point Yard office at Duluth in September 1957. While most other roads operating in the area, notably the Great Northern, were operating almost 100% with diesel locomotives during the late 1950s, the Northern Pacific was still operating a large number of well maintained steamers. This was due, in large part, to the relatively low cost of Montana's Rosebud coal for the NP. Even the cost of diesel fuel could not compete with NP's own coal. *Wayne C. Olsen*

The Pullman, Washington local switch engine, Class W-2 #1902, was one of NP's favorite form of branchline motive power. The 2-8-2 has five 40-foot grain box cars and a local caboose in tow during the early summer of 1953. *Alfred B. Butler*

The Idaho Division, along with the Rocky Mountain and Yellowstone Divisions, operated most of the Northern Pacific's large number of articulated steam locomotives. These Z Class locomotives were responsible for bumping most of the larger 2-8-2 Mikados from main line freight service in the Western mountainous areas. One of the Challenger type locomotives which called the Idaho Division home for most of its career was Z-8 #5140. The big 4-6-6-4, running light, had taken the siding at Athol, Idaho on September 22, 1957, and is once again under way. *Bruce Butler*

Below: Another Idaho Division assigned Z-8 Challenger, #5138, has worked east to Missoula on January 20, 1946, and rests between runs at the coal dock along with a host of smaller steamers during this busy time *E.T. Harley*

Challenger #5135 worked the Rocky Mountain Division for most of its career, as we see here on January 20, 1946. The huge Z-8 is working freight on Bozeman Pass, in below zero weather, as it passes the heavyweight *North Coast Limited*. The 5135 was bumped to the Idaho Division by the many new Electro-Motive freight diesel locomotives in late 1954. *E.T. Harley*

Below: Class Z-8s, 5130-5133 and 5136-5141, were originally delivered to the Idaho Division from the American Locomotive Co. in early 1943, where they worked fast freight and refer blocks between Parkwater and Yakima, Washington. They were also called to work heavy troop trains on occasion. In the mid-1950s, the 5141 was reassigned to the Yellowstone Division where it splits a pair of semaphores with a caboose-hop. The little wooden caboose in nearly lost behind the big Challenger and its huge centipede tender. *Ed Gerlits*

During the summer of 1955, #5114, a Class Z-6 Challenger hustles a westbound freight, with a cut of black NP Hart drop-bottom gondolas, down the main line through the Spokane Valley near Otis Orchards. *Alfred B. Butler*

Oil-burning Z-8 #5140, one of only two converted from coal to oil during the mid-1950s, for use on the SP&S, 5140 and 5148, is running light with an auxiliary tank across Lake Pend Oreille at Sandpoint, Idaho on September 22, 1957. This was the last time a Z-8 Challenger operated. The heavy locomotive was used to tamp down a track relocation near Noxon and Trout Creek, in western Montana. Most of these modern steam locomotives had many years of operation left when they were retired due to the arrival of scores of new road diesel locomotives. This was the last operating NP Challenger and it was very near end of the railroad's steam era. *Bruce Butler*

Northern Pacific EMD GP7 Road Switchers

Road No.	Date Built	EMD Const. No.	Dynamic Brakes	Notes & Disposition
550	2/50	10940	No	To BN 1624; converted to GP10 BN #1421, 4/75; sold to ILS, 11/86.
551	2/50	10941	No	To BN 1625; converted to GP10 BN #1426, 9/76
552	4/51	14093	No	To BN 1626; Traded-in to GE for B30-7AB, 7/82.
553	4/51	14094	No	To BN 1627; Traded-in to GE for B30-7AB, 9/82.
554	4/51	14111	No	To BN 1628; Sold to Joseph Simon & Sons, 10/82.
555	3/52	15687	No	To BN 1629; Sold to Joseph Simon & Sons, 10/82.
556	3/52	15688	No	To BN 1630; Wrecked South Seattle, 10/77; scraped by BN 12/77.
557	3/52	15689	No	To BN 1631; Traded-in to GE for B30-7AB, 9/82.
558	3/52	15690	No	To BN 1632; Traded-in to GE for B30-7AB, 10/82.
559	11/52	17479	No	To BN 1633; Traded-in to GE for B30-7AB, 9/82.
560	12/53	19031	No	To BN 1634; Sold to Joseph Simon & Sons, 10/82.
561	12/53	19032	No	To BN 1635; Traded-in to GE for B30-7AB, 9/82.
562	12/53	19033	No	To BN 1636; Sold to Hyman-Michaels, '81.
563	12/53	19034	No	To BN 1637; Traded-in to GE for B30-7AB, 9/82.
564	12/53	19035	Yes	To BN 1638; Sold to Southwestern Car Parts, 10/83.
565	12/53	19036	Yes	To BN 1639; Sold to Southwestern Car Parts, 10/83.
566	12/53	19037	Yes	To BN 1640; Sold to Precision National Corp., 12/83.
567	12/53	19038	Yes	To BN 1641; Sold to Naporano Bros. Iron & Metal Co., '81.
568	12/53	19039	Yes	To BN 1642; Sold to Naporano Bros. Iron & Metal Co., '81.
569	12/53	19040	Yes	To BN 1643; Sold to Hyman-Michaels, '81.

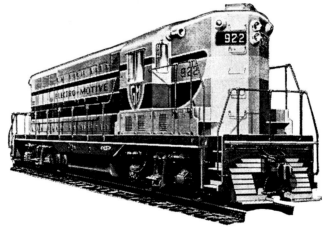

GENERAL-PURPOSE ROAD SWITCHER—This new 1500 h.p. road switching locomotive extends to branch line and local service the full savings which General Motors Diesel operation makes possible. This flexible, wide-range GP-7 unit can be used in local or mainline freight or passenger service, or both; in yard or wayside switching; in transfer, or helper service and in hump switching.

GM
GENERAL MOTORS
LOCOMOTIVES

ELECTRO-MOTIVE DIVISION

GENERAL MOTORS • LA GRANGE, ILLINOIS

Home of the Diesel Locomotive

EMD GP7s 555 and 556 were delivered in early 1952 for operation on the Washington Central Branch. Nearly identical 552-554, delivered one year earlier were purchased for operation on the Palouse and Lewiston Branch. The 555 has just been refueled and sits among many FT units. Note the GP7's original air horn location. *Montague Powell*

The NP purchased four GP7s in 1953, 560-563, with extra large 2,200-gallon fuel tanks and without dynamic brakes, for use as local freight locomotives on the many Idaho Division branchlines. Due to the large fuel tanks the four air cylinder tanks were mounted on the roof. In August 1962, GP7 #561 works Idaho Division's Walla Walla local at Eureka, Washington, with a cut of black Northern Pacific ballast hoppers. *Bruce Butler*

Idaho Division GP7 #562 is away from home as it was assigned to work with the Speno Rail Grinding Train on NP rails north of East Olympia, Washington. Track maintenance is a number one priority in maintaining fast freight and passenger schedules. The Northern Pacific owns this double track main line while extending trackage rights to the Great Northern and Union Pacific Railroads. *William J. Neill*

Baldwin VO-1000 switcher #418, photographed at Yardley in 1955, represents a conglomeration of earlier NP paint schemes. While most switchers and road-switchers had already been relettered and/or repainted by 1955, the 418 remained lettered with the pre-1954 "N.P.R." cab initials in white. Yellow "Northern Pacific" in 12-inch Roman letters was added to the side of the hood and a Monad replaced the N.P.R. above yellow cab numbers in 1953. However, yellow grab irons and hand rails, which the 418 has, was a 1955 safety enhancement. *Gayle Christen*

Electro-Motive Division introduced their 1,750-horsepower GP9 road-switcher in January 1954. The Northern Pacific purchased four GP9s, 200-203, in June for assignment to the jointly-owned, with the Union Pacific, Camas Prairie Railroad, based out of Lewiston, Idaho. The Union Pacific matched the NP by assigning GP9s UP 245-248 to the Camas Prairie in mid-1954. Both roads added an additional GP9 to the Camas Prairie about one year later, when the NP assigned 204 and the UP added their 249. This was after steam locomotives from both roads, which had been held for relief, were returned to their parent roads. During January 1955, the NP steam locomotives leased to the Camas Prairie were L-9 0-6-0 #1092 and W-1 2-8-2 #1697. NP GP9 201 rests at Lewiston, Idaho beside UP 245. *Ed Fulcomer collection*

Northern Pacific Locomotive Assignment
Tacoma Division
- January 1955 -

Locomotive No.	Class / Type		Service	Notes
35	Y	2-8-0	Switcher	Yakima
98	DE	GE 44-Ton	Switcher	South Tacoma
115-116	DE	EMD SW-9	Switcher	Seattle
400	DE	Baldwin VO-1000	Switcher	Seattle
403	DE	Baldwin VO-1000	Switcher	South Tacoma Shop
405	DE	Baldwin VO-1000	Switcher	Auburn
406	DE	Baldwin VO-1000	Switcher	Tacoma
409	DE	Baldwin VO-1000	Switcher	Seattle
412	DE	Baldwin VO-1000	Switcher	Auburn
413	DE	Baldwin VO-1000	Switcher	Tacoma
414	DE	Baldwin VO-1000	Switcher	Seattle
416-417	DE	Baldwin VO-1000	Switcher	Tacoma
419	DE	Baldwin VO-1000	Switcher	Auburn
421	DE	Baldwin VO-1000	Switcher	Centralia
422-424	DE	Baldwin VO-1000	Switcher	Seattle
425	DE	Baldwin VO-1000	Switcher	Tacoma
426	DE	Baldwin VO-1000	Switcher	Seattle
427	DE	Baldwin VO-1000	Switcher	Auburn
501	DE	Baldwin DRS 4-4-15	Passenger	
557-558	DE	EMD GP7	Freight	
602	DE	Alco HH-660	Leased	King Street Station - Seattle
650-652	DE	Baldwin VO-660	Switcher	Seattle
WWV 775	DE	Alco HH-660	Switcher	Leased from Walla Walla Valley R.R.
1041	L-9	0-6-0	Switcher	Stored - Seattle
1045	L-9	0-6-0	Switcher	Hoquiam
1049	L-9	0-6-0	Switcher	Chehalis
1052	L-9	0-6-0	Switcher	Auburn
1053, 1064	L-9	0-6-0	Switcher	Tacoma
1070	L-9	0-6-0	Switcher	Olympia
1072	L-9	0-6-0	Switcher	Centralia
1074	L-9	0-6-0	Switcher	Seattle
1076	L-9	0-6-0	Switcher	Auburn
1080	L-9	0-6-0	Switcher	Tacoma
1081	L-9	0-6-0	Switcher	Everett
1082	L-9	0-6-0	Switcher	Olympia
1083	L-9	0-6-0	Switcher	Centralia
1086	L-9	0-6-0	Switcher	Everett
1091	L-9	0-6-0	Switcher	Hoquiam
1095	L-9	0-6-0	Switcher	Tacoma
1097	L-9	0-6-0	Switcher	Seattle
1098	L-9	0-6-0	Switcher	Tacoma
1104	L-9	0-6-0	Switcher	Stored awaiting disposition
1110	L-9	0-6-0	Switcher	South Bend
1111	L-9	0-6-0	Switcher	Stored - Seattle
1118	L-9	0-6-0	Leased	King Street Station - Seattle
1122	L-9	0-6-0	Switcher	Aberdeen
1123	L-9	0-6-0	Switcher	Seattle
1126	L-9	0-6-0	Switcher	Hoquiam
1127	L-9	0-6-0	Switcher	Tacoma
1128	L-9	0-6-0	Switcher	Everett
1129	L-9	0-6-0	Leased	Simpson Logging Company
1132	L-9	0-6-0	Switcher	Tacoma
1185	G-2	0-8-0	Switcher	Shop - Auburn Roundhouse
1190	G-2	0-8-0	Switcher	Yakima
1253	Y-2	2-8-0	Switcher	Yakima
1262	Y-2	2-8-0	Switcher	Auburn
1265	Y-2	2-8-0	Switcher	Stored - Yakima
1271	Y-2	2-8-0	Switcher	Stored awaiting disposition
1274	Y-2	2-8-0	Switcher	Yakima

Northern Pacific Locomotive Assignment
Tacoma Division (Continued)
- January 1955 -

Locomotive No.	Class / Type	Service	Notes
1361, 1368-1370	S-4 4-6-0	Freight	
1372	S-4 4-6-0	Freight	Shop - Seattle Roundhouse
1373	S-4 4-6-0	Freight	Transfer
1380	S-4 4-6-0	Work	
1381	S-4 4-6-0	Freight	
1507, 1527	W 2-8-2	Freight	
1529	W 2-8-2	Freight	Stored - Tacoma
1548, 1612, 1618-1619, 1621, 1655	W 2-8-2	Freight	
1670, 1672, 1674-1675, 1677, 1679, 1682, 1690	W-1 2-8-2	Freight	
1691	W-1 2-8-2	Freight	Stored awaiting disposition
1693-1694	W-1 2-8-2	Freight	
1699	W-1 2-8-2	Freight	Stored awaiting disposition
1705-1706	W-3 2-8-2	Freight	
1708	W-3 2-8-2	Freight	Shop - Livingston
1713-1714, 1728, 1731, 1752, 1763, 1772, 1776	W-3 2-8-2	Freight	
1777	W-3 2-8-2	Freight	Stored awaiting disposition
1780, 1782-1784, 1791, 1797, 1799-1802, 1804, 1812, 1821, 1824	W-3 2-8-2	Freight	
1826	W-3 2-8-2	Freight	Helper
1829	W-3 2-8-2	Freight	
1830	W-3 2-8-2	Freight	Helper
1901	W-2 2-8-2	Freight	Helper
1905-1906, 1910-1911, 1913	W-2 2-8-2	Freight	
2152	Q-3 4-6-2	Passenger	Stored - Tacoma
2260-2261	Q-6 4-6-2	Passenger	
2262, 2264-2265	Q-6 4-6-2	Passenger	Stored awaiting disposition
2425	T 2-6-2	Switcher	Tacoma Stationary Plant
2451	T-1 2-6-2	Switcher	Seattle Stationary Plant
2453	T-1 2-6-2	Switcher	Centralia Stationary Plant
2600-2602, 2604	A 4-8-4	Freight	
2610	A 4-8-4	Passenger	
2626	A-1 4-8-4	Passenger	
5400A-B-C-D	DE FTA/FTB/FTB/FTA	Freight	
5402A-B-C-D	DE FTA/FTB/FTB/FTA	Freight	
5403A-B-C-D	DE FTA/FTB/FTB/FTA	Freight	
5404A-B-C-D	DE FTA/FTB/FTB/FTA	Freight	
5405A-B-C-D	DE FTA/FTB/FTB/FTA	Freight	
5406A-B-C-D	DE FTA/FTB/FTB/FTA	Freight	
5407A-B-C-D	DE FTA/FTB/FTB/FTA	Freight	
5409A-B-C-D	DE FTA/FTB/FTB/FTA	Freight	
5410A-B-C-D	DE FTA/FTB/FTB/FTA	Freight	
6018A-B-C-D	DE F7A/F7B/F7B/F7A	Freight	
6019A-B-C-D	DE F7A/F7B/F7B/F7A	Freight	
6020A-B-C-D	DE F7A/F7B/F7B/F7A	Freight	

Northern Pacific Railway
- Tacoma Division -

Yakama to Auburn, WA. (Main Line) . . . . 141.77 mi.
Tacoma to Seattle, WA. (Main Line) . . . . 40.17 mi.
Colorado Street Line in Seattle (Main Line) . . . . 3.19 mi.
Drawbridge Line in Tacoma (Main Line) . . . . 1.67 mi.
Tacoma to Vancouver, WA. (Main Line) . . . . 136.39 mi.
Tacoma to Tenino, WA. (Main Line) . . . . 39.52 mi.
Willbridge to Portland, OR. (Main Line) . . . . 3.56 mi.
King Street Terminal (Joint) Holgate St. to South Portal, Seattle (Main Line) . . . . . 0.98 mi.
SP&S (Joint) Vancouver, WA. to Willbridge, OR. (Main Line) . . . . 5.38 mi.
N.P. Terminal Co. of Oregon/Portland (Joint Terminal) (Main Line) . . . . 0.91 mi.
Great Northern Ry. (Leased) Seattle, WA. (Main Line) . . . . 0.04 mi.
Yakima to Moxee City, WA. (Moxee Branch) . . . . 8.73 mi.
Yakima to Naches, WA. (Naches Branch) . . . . 13.07 mi.
Brace to Tieton, WA. (Tieton Branch) . . . . 11.74 mi.
Cle Elum to Ronald, WA. (Roslyn Branch) . . . . 6.11 mi.
Palmer Junction to Meeker, WA. (Buckley Branch) . . . . 33.15 mi.
Cascade Junction to Wilkeson and Carbonado, WA. (Wilkeson Branch) . . . . 9.78 mi.
Orting to Lake Kapowsin, WA. (Orting Branch) . . . . 10.03 mi.
Kanaskat to Selleck, WA. (Green River Branch) . . . . 3.95 mi.
Black River to Woodinville, WA. (Lake Washington Belt Line) . . . . 24.13 mi.
Seattle to Sumas, WA. (Sumas Branch) . . . . 126.91 mi.
Woodinville to North Bend, WA. (Snoqualmie Branch) . . . . 38.43 mi.
Lowell to Everett, WA. (Everett Branch) . . . . 4.49 mi.
Bromart and Kruse to Edgecomb, WA. - Great Northern Ry. connections . . . . 5.02 mi.
Arlington to Darrington, WA. (Darrington Branch) . . . . 28.30 mi.
Wickersham to Bellingham, WA. (Bellingham Branch) . . . . 22.45 mi.
Lakeview to Gate, WA. (Olympia Branch) . . . . 40.36 mi.
Centralia to Aberdeen Jct. and S. Aberdeen to Markham (Grays Harbor Branch) . . 61.36 mi.
Elma to Shelton, WA. (Elma Branch) . . . . 25.88 mi.
Aberdeen Junction to Moclips, WA. (Peninsular Branch) . . . . 34.28 mi.
South Aberdeen to Cosmopolis, WA. (Cosmopolis Branch) . . . . 2.08 mi.
Chehalis Junction to South Bend, WA. (South Bend Branch) . . . . 56.65 mi.
Vancouver Junction to Yacolt, WA. (Yacolt Branch) . . . . 27.25 mi.
Trackage rights, Joint trackage and Leased Lines (Branch Lines) . . . . 66.34 mi.

Tacoma Division - Total Mileage . . . . 373.65 Main Lines - 660.49 Branch Lines

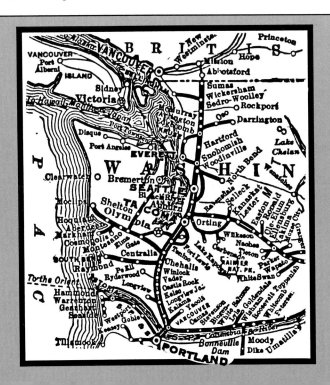

Above: NP Class L-9 steam switch engine #1070 was assigned to the Tacoma Division in January 1955, as an Olympia, Washington switcher. In August 1958, the little engine was working lumber cars at McCleary, WA. This locomotive gained notoriety on April 6, 1988, when the former NP switcher was used in commercial service to rescue several cars from a BN derailment on the ex-NP Sumas line in northern Washington. The complete story is available in the NPRHA's Winter 1989 issue of *The Mainstreeter*. *Hormer Benton*

Ten-Wheeler #1368 was one of eight 4-6-0 Class S-4s assigned to freight service on the Tacoma Division in January 1955. The locomotive is all steamed up as it moves to the coaling dock at the Hoquiam, Washington engine terminal on June 4, 1956. The Northern Pacific roundhouse at Hoquiam also served the power of the Union Pacific and Milwaukee Road, both of which operated via NP trackage rights. *Stan Kistler*

The Tacoma Division was also assigned a rather large number of 2-8-2 Mikado-type locomotives in January 1955. The well maintained #1675 represents one of a dozen Class W-1 freight locomotives on the western end of the system. *Dr. A.G. Chione*

This is perhaps the most historic photograph in this book. Class W-3 #1713, which was on the Tacoma Division in January 1955, was subsequently transferred east to the Lake Superior Division. While working the "Old Town Transfer" between Superior and Duluth, in minus 10-degree weather, on January 26, 1958, the "Mike" became the very last steam locomotive to work in revenue service on the Northern Pacific Railway. A sad day indeed! In a bit more than twelve years the Northern Pacific itself would be swallowed up in the Burlington Northern merger. *Wayne C. Olsen*

Another Mikado which was transferred east from the Tacoma Division during the late 1950s, was Class W-3 #1791. The right and left sides of this classic 2-8-2 are presented here for those modelers wishing to examine both sides of a particular locomotive. One of the most popular and successful wheel arrangements on the Northern Pacific was the 2-8-2, which occupied the number series from 1500 through 1919 and 2500 through 2505, in six classes. *Above:* The 1791 was photographed at Duluth on August 24, 1957. *Robert Bruneau - Below:* On September 30, 1957, #1791 was once again caught on film at Duluth. *Lou Schmitz*

The Northern Pacific purchased three 660-horsepower HH-660 model switchers from Alco in February 1940. They were originally numbered 1st 125-127. The 127 was initially assigned to the Idaho Division where it worked at Yardley in Spokane. During the mid-1940s, #127 was transferred to Tacoma where it worked side-by-side with #126, a sister HH-660. In December the three units were assigned new road numbers, 600-602. The 600 and 601 were subsequently sold to NP controlled Walla Walla Valley Railroad as WWV 770 and 775. Both switchers were leased back to the NP at various times and sub-leased to Seattle's King Street Station. Meanwhile, #602 was reassigned to the Fargo Division where it worked at Fargo and Dilworth. In July 1954, it was transferred to the Tacoma Division and it too, was leased to the King Street Station for passenger car switching. Except for a brief stint on the Idaho Division in mid-1955, the high-hood switcher worked at Seattle, usually shuttling passenger cars. *R.R. Wallin collection*

The Baldwin Locomotive Works, the nation's premier steam locomotive builder, produced their first production diesel locomotive, the VO-660 in 1939. The NP purchased a single VO-660, 1st 128, in April 1940. Two more, 1st 129 and 130, with a slightly different body style, were bought in March 1942. During the 1940's, all three spent time working on the Idaho and Rocky Mountain Divisions, but after 1950, they spent most of the rest of their careers assigned to the Tacoma Division working in the Seattle and Tacoma areas. The three switchers were renumbered 650-652 in December 1949 and January 1950. Ten years later, the 650 and 652 were rebuilt as electric trailer units to be mated with switchers to work the Pasco Yard. VO-660 #651, however, made it to the BN merger and was assigned, but not renumbered, BN #7. Being an orphan model, the little Baldwin switcher was sold to a used locomotive dealer soon after the merger. *James A. Adams*

One of the Baldwin Locomotive Works most successful diesel-electric models was their 1000-horsepower VO-1000 yard switcher produced between 1939 and 1946, mostly during the restrictive years of WWII. Baldwin sold a total of 548 VO-1000s during that period, with twenty-eight going to the Northern Pacific. They were originally numbered in order of purchase; 1st 109-112, 1st 119-124, 1st 153 and 154 and 1st 159-174. During December 1949 and January 1950, they were all renumbered as 400-427. During January 1955, eighteen of the twenty-eight VO-1000s plus all three VO-660s were assigned to the Tacoma Division. Baldwin #400, NP's first VO-1000, built in May 1941, was assigned to Seattle. *Matthew J. Herson*

The "standard" car-body style distinguishing the Baldwin VO-1000s featured AAR trucks and a front radiator with a slightly pointed nose. What wasn't standard were the exhaust stacks. For the most part, the stacks were offset to the left side of the hood. VO-1000 #414, assigned to Seattle, has two stacks, while Tacoma's #416 is a "four-stacker". *Above: Matthew J. Herson - Al Chione collection - Below: Gayle Christen*

Baldwin VO-1000s, 417 and 406, both assigned at Tacoma, were photographed on May 4, 1958, with portions of the obsolete paint scheme, white number plaques on their noses. Yellow was adopted in 1953, five years earlier. Baldwin #417 also displays its rather unique four stack extensions. *Montague Powell*

A more "normal" Baldwin VO-1000 diesel switcher, #421, was assigned at Centralia, Washington in January 1955, along with a pair of steam switch engines, #1072 and 1083, both Class L-9 0-6-0s. *R.R. Wallin collection*

Auburn assigned, Baldwin VO-1000 #427, has just coupled caboose NP 1145 to the rear of a long manifest. As of January 1955, there were still thirty-seven steam switch engines assigned to the Tacoma Division. Within the next three years they were all replaced with new diesel switchers from EMD. *Matthew J. Herson*

A pair of EMD GP7s, 558 and 555, along with an FT B-A set, 5409B-A, leave the main line and head for the Auburn, Washington yard. Shortly after our roster date, January 1955, GP7 555 was transferred from the Idaho Division to the Tacoma Division where it worked for many years with long time Tacoma Division GP7 residents 557 and 558. *Matthew J. Herson*

The GP7s assigned to the Tacoma Division were all equipped with large fuel tanks and usually worked with two-unit FTs in local freight service both north and south out of Auburn. The 557 was photographed at Middle Yard, Seattle. *R.R. Wallin collection*

EMD FT 5410D+C and GP7 #557 are sitting on a ready track at Seattle on May 13, 1962. By this date all eleven FT four-unit locomotive sets were assigned to the Tacoma Division, however most had been broken up into two-unit A-B locomotive sets. It was not unusual for 5410D-East to meet 5410A-West on a typical local freight. The 5410D is a historical unit. The January 1945-built machine, along with B-unit 5406C, were traded-in to GE in September 1964 for partial payment on a new locomotive by the NP. GE sold them to Hyman Michaels Co., a scrap dealer, who resold them in 1965, to the Sonora-Baja California R.R. in Sonora, Mexico. Thus they became the world's last operating FT units. The locomotives that beagn the demise of steam in America. *Montague Powell*

A perfect A-B-B-A set of FT units, 5407A-B-C-D, assigned to the Tacoma Division, is hustling an eastbound freight past the Plains, Montana depot on the Idaho Division in July 1964. Shortly the manifest will enter the Rocky Mountain Division at Paradise. *Bruce Butler*

Northern Pacific EMD FT Freight Locomotives
- January 1955 -

Previous Road No.	Road No. 1955	Model	Date Built	EMD Const. No.	Notes & Disposition
6000A (1st)	5400A	EMD FTA	2/44	1978	Traded-in to EMD for SD45 4/68.
6000B (1st)	5400B	EMD FTB	2/44	1984	Traded-in to GE for U25C 8/64.
6000C (1st)	5400C	EMD FTB	2/44	1985	Traded-in to EMD for SD45 3/67.
6000D (1st)	5400D	EMD FTA	2/44	1979	Traded-in to EMD for SD45 2/67.
6001A (1st)	5401A	EMD FTA	3/44	1980	Traded-in to GE for U33C 7/69.
6001B (1st)	5401B	EMD FTB	3/44	1986	Traded-in to EMD for SD45 4/67.
6001C (1st)	5401C	EMD FTB	3/44	1987	Traded-in to GE for U25C 9/64.
6001D (1st)	5401D	EMD FTA	3/44	1981	Traded-in to GE for U33C 7/69.
6002A (1st)	5402A	EMD FTA	4/44	1982	Traded-in to GE for U28C 8/66.
6002B (1st)	5402B	EMD FTB	4/44	1988	Traded-in to GE for U28C 8/66.
6002C (1st)	5402C	EMD FTB	4/44	1989	Traded-in to EMD for SD45 2/67.
6002D (1st)	5402D	EMD FTA	4/44	1983	Traded-in to GE for U25C 4/64.
6003A (1st)	5403A	EMD FTA	6/44	2557	Traded-in to EMD for SD45 5/70 by BN.
6003B (1st)	5403B	EMD FTB	6/44	2565	Traded-in to EMD for SD45 3/68.
6003C (1st)	5403C	EMD FTB	6/44	2569	Traded-in to GE for U25C 9/65.
6003D (1st)	5403D	EMD FTA	6/44	2561	Traded-in to EMD for SD45 4/67.
6004A (1st)	5404A	EMD FTA	7/44	2558	Traded-in to GE for U25C 10/65.
6004B (1st)	5404B	EMD FTB	7/44	2566	Traded-in to GE for U25C 10/65.
6004C (1st)	5404C	EMD FTB	7/44	2570	Traded-in to EMD for SD45 6/70 by BN.
6004D (1st)	5404D	EMD FTA	7/44	2562	Traded-in to GE for U25C 8/64.
6005A (1st)	5405A	EMD FTA	8/44	2559	Traded-in to EMD for SD45 2/67.
6005B (1st)	5405B	EMD FTB	8/44	2567	Traded-in to EMD for SD45 2/67.
6005C (1st)	5405C	EMD FTB	8/44	2571	Traded-in to EMD for SD45 4/68.
6005D (1st)	5405D	EMD FTA	8/44	2563	Traded-in to EMD for SD45 3/67.
6006A (1st)	5406A	EMD FTA	10/44	2560	Traded-in to EMD for SD45 3/68.
6006B (1st)	5406B	EMD FTB	10/44	2568	Traded-in to GE for U33C 7/69.
6006C (1st)	5406C	EMD FTB	10/44	2572	Traded-in to GE for U25C 9/64, to SBC, Sonora, Mex. #2203B.
6006D (1st)	5406D	EMD FTA	10/44	2564	Traded-in to EMD for SD45 4/68.
6007A (1st)	5407A	EMD FTA	11/44	2836	Traded-in to GE for U28C 8/66.
6007B (1st)	5407B	EMD FTB	11/44	2844	Traded-in to GE for U33C 7/69.
6007C (1st)	5407C	EMD FTB	11/44	2848	Traded-in to GE for U28C 8/66.
6007D (1st)	5407D	EMD FTA	11/44	2840	Traded-in to GE for U28C 8/66.
6008A (1st)	5408A	EMD FTA	11/44	2837	Traded-in to GE for U25C 9/65.
6008B (1st)	5408B	EMD FTB	11/44	2845	Traded-in to GE for U25C 9/65.
6008C (1st)	5408C	EMD FTB	11/44	2849	Traded-in to GE for U28C 8/66.
6008D (1st)	5408D	EMD FTA	11/44	2841	Traded-in to GE for U25C 9/65.
6009A (1st)	5409A	EMD FTA	1/45	2838	Traded-in to EMD for SD45 5/70 by BN.
6009B (1st)	5409B	EMD FTB	1/45	2846	Traded-in to EMD for SD45 5/70 by BN.
6009C (1st)	5409C	EMD FTB	1/45	2850	Traded-in to EMD for SD45 4/68.
6009D (1st)	5409D	EMD FTA	1/45	2842	Traded-in to EMD for SD45 6/70 by BN.
6010A (1st)	5410A	EMD FTA	1/45	2839	Traded-in to GE for U25C 3/64.
6010B (1st)	5410B	EMD FTB	1/45	2847	Traded-in to GE for U25C 3/64.
6010C (1st)	5410C	EMD FTB	1/45	2851	Traded-in to EMD for SD45 5/70 by BN.
6010D (1st)	5410D	EMD FTA	1/45	2843	Traded-in to GE for U25C 9/64, to SBC, Sonora, Mex. #2203A.

Northern Pacific 5402, a pristine, freshly painted four-unit FT locomotive set was at the Pasco, Washington hump yard dedication in July 1955. *Walter Oberst - Bruce Butler collection*

Cosmetically, Northern Pacific FTs were "standardized" in installments. The 5405 has had some improvements added but there were more to come. First, during the late 1940s, the original small number boards were replaced with larger boards at 45-degree angles for better visibility. Yellow 6000 series, 12-inch Gothic numerals were added to the sides of the cab units near the rear. In December 1949 and January 1950, the entire group was renumbered from the 6000 to 5400 series, representing the horsepower of a four-unit consist. During the mid-1940s, *Main Street of the Northwest* was added on each side of the booster units. Then, non-skid treads were affixed across the nose just below the windshields and grab irons were attached just above the windshields. A single grab was also added on each side of the nose just below the windshields. Later the "Stimsonite" reflectorized number buttons on the top of the front door were removed. Next, lift rings were added during the early 1950s. Then ladder stirrups were affixed on the right side of the nose, just behind the number board enabling maintenance personnel to clean the windshields with much more ease. In 1954, 12-inch numbers were painted on the sides of the booster units, the letters A though D were added behind the locomotive number and the lettering around the Monad was changed from "Northern Pacific" to "Northern Pacific Railway". The "pine tree" painted on the nose was modified, as seen above, to bypass the number boards. During the late 1950s, twin sealed-beam headlights were installed in the nose door, where the reflectorized number plates had been located. A red and clear oscillating headlight was installed in the original light housing. Note the 5405 has a radio antenna but the "Radio Equipped" emblem has not yet been added. The horns were also changed on some of the FTA units. The 5405 locomotive set is at Missoula on July 29, 1955. *Montague Powell*

Northern Pacific's Portland to Seattle time freight #1-667, rolls through a trademark of the Pacific Northwest, a late afternoon rain. Crew members from a local road switcher watch the passing of the freight with four units of FT #5400 at Chehalis, Washington on NP's double track Portland - Seattle main line. *Gil Hulin*

Northern Pacific, unlike most other roads, kept the drawbar coupling between their FT cab and booster pairs. Notice the tight spacing between the 5410A+B and the greater spacing between the booster units 5410B and 5402C. The locomotive set of 5410A-B and 5402C-D is at Seattle on May 13, 1962, awaiting a call.
Montague Powell photo - Matthew J. Herson collection

Diesel locomotive set 5405D-C-B-A is awaiting a new crew at Missoula, Montana on July 29, 1955. Notice, the large unit numbers, 5405B + 5405C, have not yet been applied to the booster units. All of the FT locomotives, except 5401 and 5408, were assigned to the Tacoma Division in 1955. The two Rocky Mountain Division FT locomotives, 5401 and 5408, soon joined the other nine FT sets, with Auburn as their maintenance point. *Montague Powell*

June 30, 1957, found Northern Pacific's original freight locomotive at Auburn, the road's first major western diesel locomotive service facilities. Originally numbered 1st 6000, this set, along with 6001 and 6002, was built in February 1944, and signaled the beginning of the end for NP's steam locomotive fleet. *M.W. Anderson*

Even though the Northern Pacific FTs were among some of the last built, February 1944 through January 1945, the entire fleet stayed intact until late 1964, when specific units began being used as partial payment for new second generation diesel locomotives. They were traded-in to both EMD and GE. The Tacoma Division was these veteran locomotives last assignment. Four of the survivors, led by 5400A, NP's first FT, works tonnage through Kent, Washington on October 9, 1967. *Matthew J. Herson*

One of the arguments some of Northern Pacific's management made for not purchasing more road freight locomotives during the mid-1940s, was the fact that they were worried about fluctuations in the cost of diesel fuel and the possibility that the Federal Government might restrict supplies during WWII. Another reason was that the NP owned huge reserves of low-grade coal at Colstrip, Montana, which fed their modern fleet of steam locomotives. *Bruce Butler*

Three F7s and an F9A kick up dust as they accelerate past a train order signal at Minneapolis after uncoupling from their manifest. During the mid-1950s, the NP began mixing their freight units and generally did away with operating four units as a single locomotive. This promoted much greater flexibility when despatchers built motive power consists. A "locomotive" could be put together using two, three or four units as needed. *R.R. Wallin coll.*

One of the three F7 locomotive sets assigned to the Tacoma Division for maintenance in 1955, 6018, is leaving Rocky Canyon as it descends Bozeman Pass in western Montana on October 3rd. Making freight #603 rather interesting is five deadhead heavyweight Pullman sleeping cars on the headend. *Warren McGee*

Five F7s make up this freight consist at Mandan, North Dakota, after F7A #6019A was added on the point of the 6011 A-B-C-D, a four-unit F7 locomotive set. Notice the two different types of air horns on these F7As, as well as on the 6018A and 6019D, below. Once again demonstrating for modelers that all units are not always identical. *Jerry Quinn*

A pair of F7As, 6018A and 6019D, get a short local freight underway from Auburn. It was rather unusual, but prototype, for just two NP cab units to be operated without a booster unit. *Matthew J. Herson - Al Chione collection*

Train #602, with F7 locomotive set #6018, running as Extra-6018-East, is 3-miles east of Logan, Montana on November 8, 1954. The freight is operating on the "Low Line" in the Gallatin Valley, avoiding the 1% grades of the "High Line" to Bozeman, which was abandoned in 1957. *Warren McGee*

Tacoma Division's F7 locomotive set, #6020A-B-C-D, with a westbound time freight, is passing the Hauser depot in eastern Washington in August 1955. Notice the collection of Great Northern, Milwaukee Road and NP stock cars on the headend, a type of freight that all too soon would be taken over by cattle trucks. The photographer caught his son, a young Bruce Butler, a railfan and photographer in his own right, at a photo location, atop a cut of ice bunker refrigerator cars, another type of railroad car gone from the rail scene. Those were the days! *Alfred B. Butler*

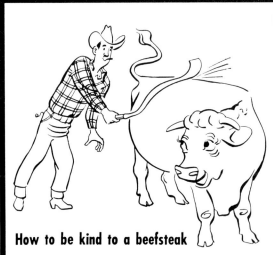

How to be kind to a beefsteak

Extra-5404A-West, with a two-unit FT locomotive, works a long freight of empty lumber box cars returning to the Pacific Northwest. It's near Christmas, a very cold December evening, as the westbound train operates through the beautiful, snowy countryside of northern Idaho, near Algoma. *Bruce Butler*

MAIN STREET OF THE NORTHWEST

- Northern Pacific Color Pictorial - Volume 2 -

Featuring the 1964 Roster, after all First Generation Diesels had arrived, prior to the Second Generation.

- Don't miss all of the action from Four Ways West Publications -

NORTHERN PACIFIC
Steam Locomotive Roster
- January 1955 -

Type	Class	Road Numbers - Jan. 1955 (Total Locomotives Originally in Class)	1955 Total
2-8-0	Y-1	21, 23-28 (17-29)	7
2-8-0	Y	31, 33-36, 42 (30-43)	6
0-6-0	L-7	1031 (1020-1035)	1
0-6-0	L-9	1040-1041, 1043, 1045, 1049, 1051-1053, 1057-1058, 1061-1065, 1070-1072, 1074, 1076-1077, 1080-1083, 1086, 1088, 1091-1093, 1095, 1097-1098, 1104, 1110-1115, 1118-1120, 1122-1123, 1126-1129, 1132 (1040-1143)	48
0-6-0	L-10	1160-1169 (1160-1169)	10
0-8-0	G-1	1170-1173 (1170-1173)	4
0-8-0	G-2	1174-1193 (1174-1193)	20
2-8-0	Y-3	1201, 1213 (1200-1213)	2
2-8-0	Y-2	1250, 1253-1254, 1262, 1264-1265, 1271, 1274 (1250-1279)	8
4-6-0	S-4	1351, 1353-1356, 1358-1362, 1365-1366, 1368-1370, 1372-1377, 1379-1382, 1387 (1350-1389)	26
2-8-2	W	1504, 1506-1507, 1514, 1516, 1520-1521, 1527, 1529-1530, 1533, 1535-1536, 1544-1546, 1548, 1550-1552, 1554, 1558, 1561-1562, 1565, 1568, 1573-1581, 1585, 1588, 1591-1592, 1595, 1597, 1605-1606, 1609, 1612-1613, 1616, 1618-1619, 1621, 1623-1624, 1627, 1632, 1634, 1638-1639, 1642, 1646-1647, 1649, 1651, 1655, 1657, 1659 (1500-1659)	66
2-8-2	W-1	1660-1670, 1672-1675, 1677, 1679, 1681-1688, 1690-1691, 1693-1694, 1696-1697, 1699 (1660-1699)	32
2-8-2	W-3	1705-1715, 1717-1722, 1725, 1728-1729, 1731, 1733-1743, 1746, 1749, 1752, 1758, 1761, 1763-1764, 1767-1770, 1772-1774, 1776-1778, 1780-1784, 1787-1795, 1797-1802, 1804-1812, 1814-1822, 1824-1827, 1829-1834 (1700-1834)	97
2-8-2	W-5	1836-1843, 1845-1847, 1849, 1852, 1854-1859 (1835-1859)	19
2-8-2	W-2	1901-1902, 1904-1906, 1908, 1910-1916, 1918-1919 (1900-1919)	15
4-6-2	Q-3	2150-1253, 2160, 2162-2164 (2148-2170)	7
4-6-2	Q-4	2180, 2182-2183, 2192, 2200, 2202, 2212, 2220, 2222-2223 (2177-2224)	10
4-6-2	Q-5	2228, 2232, 2238, 2245 (2226-2245)	4
4-6-2	Q-6	2246, 2253-2254, 2256-2257, 2260-2262, 2264-2265 (2246-2265)	10
2-6-2	T	2305, 2315, 2321, 2385-2386, 2407, 2413, 2416, 2419, 2424-2425, 2430, 2434, 2446 (2300-2449)	14
2-6-2	T-1	2450-2451, 2453-2457, 2459-2460, 2463, 2465-2467 (2450-2467)	13
2-8-2	W-4	2500-2505 (2500-2505)	6
4-8-4	A	2600-2602, 2604, 2610 (2600-2611)	5
4-8-4	A-1	2626 (2626)	1
4-8-4	A-2	2650-2651, 2656-2658 (2650-2659)	5
4-8-4	A-3	2661, 2663-2664, 2666-2667 (2660-2667)	5
4-8-4	A-4	2670-2673, 2675-2677 (2670-2677)	7
4-8-4	A-5	2680-2689 (2680-2689)	10
2-8-8-4	Z-5	5001-5002, 5004-5007 (5000-5011)	6
4-6-6-4	Z-6	5100-5104, 5106-5109, 5111-5120 (5100-5120)	19
4-6-6-4	Z-7	5121-5126 (5121-5126)	6
4-6-6-4	Z-8	5130-5149 (5130-5149)	20

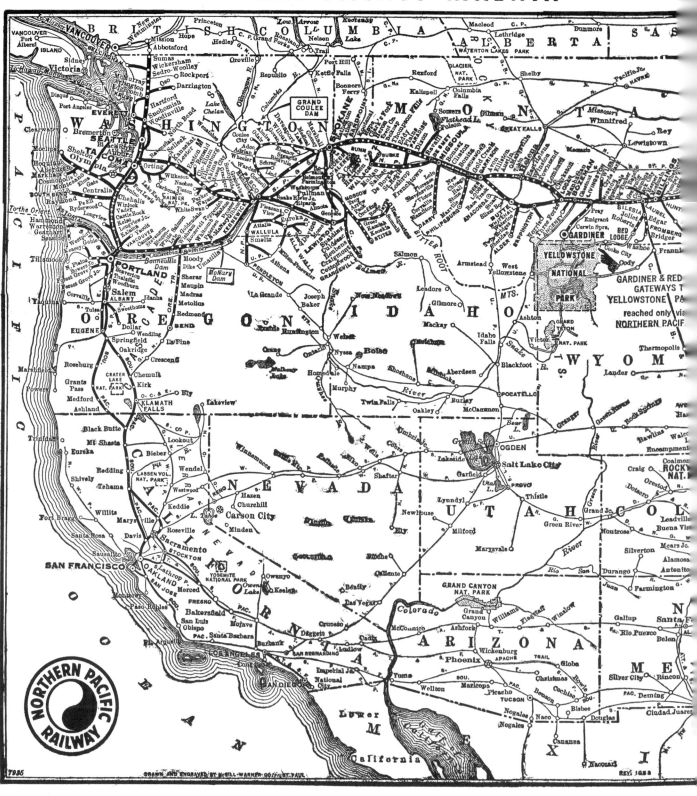